DAVID FERMER

Coast to Coast

CORNELSEN
ENGLISH
LIBRARY

Cornelsen

CORNELSEN **ENGLISH** LIBRARY
David Fermer · From Coast to Coast

Verlagsredaktion
Neil Porter

Umschlaggestaltung
hawemannundmosch, Konzeption und Gestaltung, Berlin

Titelbild
© Mauritius images / Ryan Jorgensen / Alamy

Karte
© Fotolia / dikobrazik

Layout & technische Umsetzung
Annika Preyhs für Buchgestaltung +, Berlin

www.cornelsen.de

1. Auflage, 6. Druck 2021

Alle Drucke dieser Auflage sind inhaltlich unverändert
und können im Unterricht nebeneinander verwendet werden.

Druck: AZ Druck und Datentechnik GmbH, Kempten

ISBN 978-3-06-035271-5

PEFC zertifiziert
Dieses Produkt stammt aus nachhaltig
bewirtschafteten Wäldern und kontrollierten
Quellen.

www.pefc.de

PEFC/04-31-2260

CONTENTS

Foreword   **5**

Part One   **9**

Part Two   **71**

Bibliography & References   **110**

Vocabulary   **111**

Check your understanding   **127**

FOREWORD

This story is set at the end of 2013, in the time following the introduction of Operation Sovereign Borders by the Australian government. Also known as the "stop the boats" policy, Operation Sovereign Borders promised to turn back all
5 immigrants trying to enter Australia illegally by boat.

Around the same time, the Regional Resettlement Arrangement with Papua New Guinea was signed. As a result, two Regional Processing Centres (RPCs) run by Australian companies were opened on the Pacific islands of
10 Manus and the Republic of Nauru. All illegal arrivals were to be sent to these RPCs while their asylum applications were being processed. Both Manus Island and Nauru are not a part of Australia. Manus Island belongs to Papua New Guinea. The Republic of Nauru is a sovereign state and the
15 third smallest country in the world.

The Regional Resettlement Arrangement stopped illegal maritime arrivals who were given asylum (that is "real" refugees) from entering Australia. Instead, they were sent to Papua New Guinea or the Republic of Nauru, where they
20 would live in a resettlement program paid for by Australia.

Although the Australia government has come under a lot of international criticism for its "stop the boats" policy, Operation Sovereign Borders was extremely effective in stopping the flow of illegal maritime arrivals to Australia, resulting in
25 a drop in deaths at sea, one of the main arguments used by the government to justify the policy. The offshore processing and re-settlement plan is funded by the Department of

Immigration and Border Protection (DIBP) to an estimated cost of around a billion Australian dollars per year.

Although journalists have not been allowed to visit the RPCs, human rights organizations have collected eyewitness accounts in order to document conditions in the camps. 5 Many letters, written by refugees themselves, form the basis of this story. Most recently, inquiries into the sexual abuse of women and children in the RPCs have put the Australian government under further pressure. At the time of writing this book, however, both policies are still in place and hun- 10 dreds of people are still detained on these Pacific islands. For further references, see the reading list at the end of this book.

David Fermer

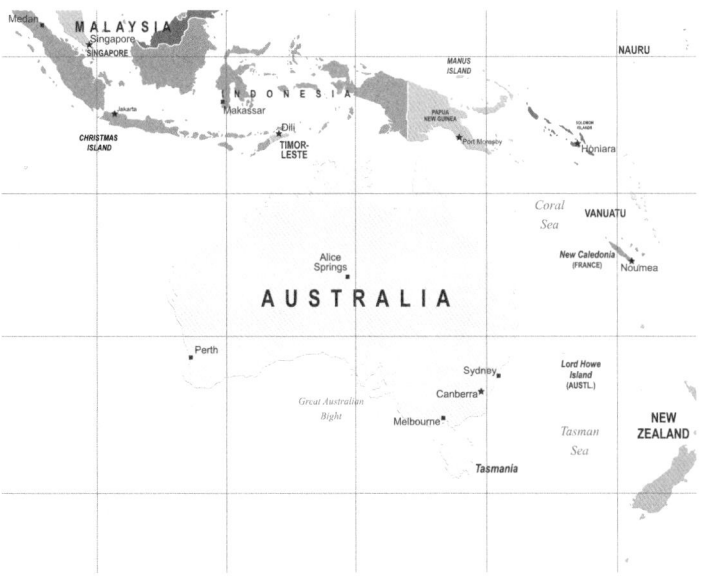

Map of Australia showing the Regional Processing Centres on Christmas Island (Australia), Manus Island (Papua New Guinea) and in the Republic of Nauru.

PART ONE

1

Do you know what hell is? Hell is 50 degrees in the shade. Hell is not being able to sleep at night because you are afraid. Hell is sweat, thirst, hunger, sickness, waiting, hoping things will change, but not knowing when they will. Hell is feeling hope
5 *dying slowly inside of you like a plant without water. Hell is where I am.*

*

When I was a kid, Dad used to say heaven is an Australian beach, and I reckon he's right. The beaches around Darwin are beautiful: the endless sky, like the promise of adventure,
10 the breeze of the salty air, the soft sand against your feet, the border between land and sea.

We have two beaches in Darwin: Mindli and Casuarina. Mindli is where you go to party. Casuarina is where you go when you want to be alone. I go there when life is getting me
15 down, when school is shitty, or something is bugging me – or when I have an argument with my dad.

"When are you gonna stop treating school like a goddam holiday camp, Cooper?" (I've heard that a hundred times.) "Get a haircut!" (At least I've *got* hair, Dad.) "If you wanna
20 throw your life away that's fine by me, but let me give you one word of advice: stop hanging around with losers like Graham Barton!"

Just some of the things he said to me when he got back from work yesterday.

Of course, I had answers like: "If Graham is a loser and his parents voted for you at the last aldermen elections, what does that say about the people who vote for you, Dad?"

Get Dad onto the subject of politics, he backs off faster than a dog caught napping by a snake. He's campaigning to 5 become mayor of Darwin, and politics is a sensitive issue between us.

Once I've had enough of hearing about what a waste of space I am, I go to the beach to clear my head. One more year of school, then I'm out of this place. Sydney, Melbourne, 10 Perth. There's no town north of Darwin.

I was walking along the beach as the sun went down. An orange blaze cut through the clouds, sending golden shimmers onto the water. How could anyone not feel good here? You can be at rock-bottom, the worst day of your life, but 15 when you look at the sundown over the Timor Sea, you just know everything's going to be all right.

It was then that I saw him: a brown lump on the sand, dark against the orange of the sun. At first I didn't know what it was. A baby croc? A tree trunk? It was only when I took a 20 few steps closer that I saw it was a person. He was huddled up like a baby, his knees under his chin, his arms around his legs, his T-shirt torn and dirty. I had to walk around him to get a look at his face: black hair speckled with white sand; slender, Asian eyes. He looked around my age. 25

"Hey! Are you all right?" I put my hand on his back. He didn't move. I shook him harder. "Hey! Wake up, mate!"

No reaction.

I panicked. *Jesus, this guy is friggin' dead!* I already had my phone in my hand, ready to call Triple Zero, but my fingers 30 froze on the keys. I was shaking.

I put my phone away and got down to my knees. I took a deep breath and tried to focus. I've done a lot of First Aid courses in my time. I know the routine. *First check to see if he's breathing. If not, do CPR.* I bent down and put my face up
5   to his nostrils. I could feel his breath on the skin of my cheek.

"Hey, mate, can you hear me?"

I tried to check his pulse, but I couldn't find it. I rolled him onto his back and grabbed his legs. I started shaking them like I was trying to rip them off. *Get some blood back into that
10 head of his! The brain needs oxygen!*

It was then that he opened his eyes. He stared straight up at me, me standing above him, holding his feet under my arms, shaking his legs. He didn't seem in the least bit surprised.

15 I dropped his legs. "Are you all right?"

He turned his head and looked from left to right. "Where I?" he asked – two words that sounded like a distant dream.

"You're in Australia, mate. You're gonna be fine."

2

There is no such thing as time on Nauru. Each day lasts a year.
20 *Each night feels like eternity.*

At night I do not sleep. Sleep is too dangerous. I close my eyes. I listen to the silence, but if I fall asleep, I wake up immediately. I live in a tent with thirty other men, men who are older than me, men who are here on their own, men with needs.

25 *Every night I go outside and walk from 11pm to 1am. It is the only time I can find peace. The camp is quiet at night. The air is fresher. They gave us fans to help us cool down the tents,*

but during the day the electricity often stops, so the fans do not help us.

Outside, in the coolness of the night, I think and think, but I cannot find a solution. I do not understand why they are doing this to us. Why do we have to suffer so much at the end of our 5 *journey? We have been through so much. We left our homes because of suffering. Why are we being punished for making this journey?*

The people who sent us here, they have forgotten that we are humans. 10

＊

His name was Bashir, that much he could tell me. He came from Afghanistan. He spoke a few words of English, not much, but enough to say he'd been on a boat and that the boat had sunk in a storm. He'd held onto a life jacket and must have drifted around in the sea for hours. It's a miracle 15 the sharks didn't get him. Or the crocs on the beach.

We sat there together on the sand for a while, watching the sun disappear behind the sea, and I knew from the moment I met him that I liked this guy. There was something intelligent in his eyes. He didn't say much, but I understood 20 him. Occasionally he smiled, a dreamy smile, as if he couldn't quite believe what was going on, as if he was surprised to be alive. A couple of his front teeth were missing. He looked like a little kid or an old homeless guy. His face kept changing, sometimes young, sometimes old, like two people moving 25 between two different worlds. I figured he was both at the same time – young and old. I guessed that was why he was here.

What now? I kept thinking. *What am I going to do with this guy?* What do you do with an illegal immigrant washed up on a beach in Australia?

"Are you hungry?" I asked him.

5   He didn't understand. I used my hands to show him what I meant.

He nodded. "Yes. Hungry," he said.

I took him to Joey's near the university and bought him some spare ribs and chips with lots of ketchup. He ate the
10 stuff like he hadn't eaten for days. I guess he probably hadn't.

People kept looking at us.

"Slow down, Bashir," I told him. "Take it easy."

He seemed to understand. He saw the people staring.

After he'd finished his meal, we headed back to Rapid
15 Creek. It was getting late. I told him to wait for me on the footbridge. "I'll be back in fifteen minutes." I gave him my watch and showed him when I'd be back.

I walked home and took the back door into the house. I went upstairs quietly, making sure no one saw me. Dad was
20 out. Mum was in the living room, working on her laptop with the TV on. My little sister was in bed.

I put some fresh clothes into a bag, took some soap and deodorant out of the bathroom. A toothbrush, toothpaste, my old sleeping bag. I went back downstairs and took some
25 milk out of the fridge, a can of spam, a tin opener, some biscuits. Don't ask me how I did it without Mum seeing me, but I did. I guess I can be pretty sneaky at times.

I was back on the footbridge in no time. Bashir looked relieved to see me.

30 "Come with me," I told him.

I took him to the hut where Dad keeps his canoe and fishing gear. It's around the back of the Surf Life Saving Club on Casuarina beach where Dad is a member. They let him build it when I was a kid, back in the days when we used to go canoeing together. It's not really official, but they let him 5 build it anyway. It's kind of hidden away in the mangroves. No one in the Club has ever really noticed it. You can't even see it from the beach. It was the perfect place for Bashir.

I opened the hut and told Bashir he could stay here. I gave him the sleeping bag and showed him what I'd brought with 10 me. He didn't say anything. He just nodded and flashed that dreamy smile of his that was fast becoming familiar to me.

It was hard to leave him there that night alone, but I guess anything was better than lying half-dead on a beach. I told him I would come around after school the next day. I told 15 him not to go out. "You have to be careful," I said. "No one can see you here." I think he understood.

I went home and slipped back into the house. Dad was home. I could hear him talking to Mum in the living room. I called out to them, saying I was going to bed. I didn't want 20 them asking any awkward questions.

Up in my room I realized how tired I was. I went straight to bed, but I couldn't sleep. My mind was racing, a thousand questions shooting through my head like a pinball machine. It was strange. Bashir and I were complete strangers, but 25 now we were connected: me in my bed, the TV humming downstairs, my sister fast asleep in the room next door, and Bashir down at the beach, sleeping on the floor of our hut.

I was still awake when my parents turned off the TV and came upstairs. I heard them walk past my door. One of them 30 stopped, I guess Mum, to listen for a moment. I didn't move a muscle until I heard her walk away.

<h1 style="text-align:center">3</h1>

*There are many animals here I do not know. There are scor-
pions and crabs which come into our tents at night. There are*
5 *lizards, spiders and cockroaches. We have mice, rats and mos-
quitoes. They live off us like parasites.*

*Yesterday I was on the toilet when a snake came in through
a hole in the wall. It moved over my bare feet. Its skin was warm
and dry, the scales as smooth as ice. I wanted to jump up and*
10 *run away, but I stopped myself. I stayed very still until the snake
moved on and disappeared out of the cubicle.*

Sometimes I think they put snakes in our tents to scare us.

*

School next day was like a waiting game. Waiting for the day
to end, waiting to get to the beach. I'd left my watch with
15 Bashir the night before, so I spent all day discovering clocks
on the walls that I'd never even seen before, watching their
hands creep slowly by, checking my phone under the shadow
of desks. Time can be your worst enemy when you want it to
go by quickly.

20 I couldn't concentrate on anything that day. The teachers'
voices sounded like faraway echoes. Everything I wrote was
like someone else was writing it for me. Me? I was somewhere else. The only person I spoke to was Kate.

"I need to talk to you," I told her in the morning.

"Sure. What's up?"

"Not now. At break. Alone."

I didn't mean to scare her, but I know I did. God knows what she thought. Trouble with my dad? Trouble with the law? Trouble was written all over my face. She kept looking 5 at me during lessons, sneaking glances between heads and shoulders, trying to read what had happened from my eyes, but I know how to keep my face blank.

We met at break around the back of the school. It stinks around there because of the trash cans, so you can usually 10 count on being alone.

"What is it?" Kate asked me.

I've known Kate all my life. We went to the same kindergarten, the same primary school, now we attend the same secondary school. We're like brother and sister. 15

I told her about finding Bashir the night before, about how I'd given him food and let him sleep in the hut. I told her the few things I knew about him, that he came from Afghanistan, that his family lived in Pakistan, that he was on the boat that had sunk off the coast near Darwin. Kate listened 20 to me with that listening face of hers, the way she does when things are serious. When I finished, she turned to me and said, "Are you crazy?"

It wasn't quite the response I was expecting, but it didn't surprise me. Kate is straighter than the Stuart Highway. 25

"You have to talk to your dad," she said.

"You know what my dad would do. He'd go straight to the cops."

"Yeah, right," she agreed. "He would. Because it happens to be the right thing!" 30

"You should have seen him, Kate. He was half dead."

"You can't help him, Cooper."

"Dad can't help him either."

Kate rolled her eyes. "It's the law, Coop. You can't just hide an illegal immigrant. At least tell your mum."

5 "As if she's any different!"

"You can't do this, Cooper."

I knew Kate wasn't going to like what I'd done, but I still had to tell her. She's is the only person I trust. We might be different, but we have a common history. Kate has always 10 been there for me. But helping illegal immigrants? That was a step too far for her.

"This is too big for you, Cooper," she said. "You're gonna get into trouble."

Kate looked up to the sky, pulling her thoughts back to 15 the confines of her own mind. I followed her line of gaze. Above us a sea eagle was drawing circles in the sky, waiting for us to leave. I had no answers, but it didn't really matter now. Bashir was here. And Bashir was alone.

"You're gonna have to do something," Kate said as the bell 20 rang to end break. "He can't stay at your beach hut forever."

"Maybe," I said, but I wasn't ready to give up yet.

4

A couple of days ago a woman from RPC 3 gave birth at the local hospital. They brought her back to the camp today with her baby. When I saw the child in her arms, I asked myself: 25 *what nationality is the baby? The parents are from Myanmar, so is the baby Burmese? The child was born in Nauru, so does that make the baby Nauruan? Then again, this camp is run by an Australian company, and we are here because the Australian government sent us here, so does that make the baby Australian? Or maybe the baby is nothing at all? No passport, no nationality. Born in nowhere, belonging to no one?*

All I know is that it's not the baby's fault it was born here. I 5
hope it finds a home soon.

*

After school I went home to get more food. No one was there so I could move around the house freely. I grabbed a sports bag from my room and filled it with stuff from the kitchen, careful only to take so much that nobody would notice: half 10 a packet of my sister's cereals, a can of pineapple chunks, some more biscuits, nothing that anyone would miss.

I was just about to leave when Dad's voice hit me out of the blue: "Hi, Coop!"

I spun around, eyes wide like the thief caught red-handed 15 who I was. Dad was leaning against the doorframe, his tie loose around his neck. He was home earlier than I expected.

"You were out late last night," he said in a voice that sounded like it was trying to be friendly. "Where were you?"

I had no choice but to lie, and years of experience have 20 taught me that a lie which tells half the truth is always the better lie.

"Down at the beach," I said.

"With Graham?"

I hesitated. "No. Alone." 25

Dad stepped into the kitchen and looked at the bag. "What's that?"

"I'm going around to Kate's to do some project work," I said, thinking on my feet. Kate is always my best alibi. Dad loves her.

"And Kate needs bananas?"

5 I looked at the bag. A bunch of bananas was sticking out of the open zip.

"The project is all about … bananas," I said.

Dad laughed as if he could see straight through me but for some reason didn't care. He wanted to avoid an argu-
10 ment, that much was clear.

"Do you want a drink?" he asked, going to the fridge.

"Na, I'm fine, thanks." I pushed the bananas back into the bag, zipped it up and checked my watch. It was gone four. I was running late.

15 "Listen, Coop," Dad said, taking out a soda. "You and I haven't been getting along too well recently. I think it's time we talked."

Not now, Dad! Please! I really don't need this right now.

"It's no big deal," I said, throwing the bag over my shoul-
20 der. I thought if I gave him a convincing display of indifference, Dad would let it go.

"Well it is to me," Dad insisted. "You're important, son, and I want us to get along."

He put his hand on my shoulder. It felt strange – familiar
25 and far away at the same time. I couldn't remember the last time he touched me.

"I know this campaign is difficult for you," he continued. "It's difficult for all of us. For your mom, for your sister, for me."

30 I had planned to take some milk, but I decided to leave that now. All I wanted was for Dad to stop talking.

"I've gotta go, Dad."

I took a step past him, heading for the door, but Dad held me back. "Wait a sec! You can't just leave!"

I can't?

"Family is important, Coop. It's the most important thing 5 in the world. Don't you want us to get along?"

"We would get along a lot better if you just let me go."

Dad held onto my arm. He looked at the bag, then back to me, and forced a smile onto his face. An act of mind over matter. 10

"All right, Coop," he said, his voice softer. He let go of my arm. "You go if you have to, mate. I don't want to hold you up." I took a step to the door. He was trying to sound casual again. "Maybe you and I can go fishing some time, what d'you say? Just like old times. You and me. A boy's day out. 15 I bet there are plenty of fish out there this time of year. We could –"

I didn't hear his last words. I was out of the kitchen and hurrying down the hall. I didn't look back. Out the front door. Down the steps. Along the drive. I couldn't believe my luck. 20 I had taken a bag full of food without Dad even asking me what I was doing with it! Bananas for Kate? Yeah, mate! And kangaroos do karate!

"Hey, Coop!" Dad's voice rang out again. I slipped out of the front gate and turned to close it. Dad was standing 25 on the porch. "I love you, son!" he called out, and his words stabbed me like a knife. "You take care of yourself!"

5

Some days we have no water here. There is no drinking water, no water for the showers. When we take a shower, the guards tell us we have one minute to wash ourselves, no more. They turn off the water when the time is up. But the water trickles ₅ *out of the shower so it is not possible to wash your whole body in the time they give you.*

The more people who come here, the less water there is. People grow weak. The place gets dirtier. The toilets smell. The tents are covered in mould. No one can be healthy here. There ₁₀ *are holes in the roof of our tent. When it rains, we get water inside. The mould is black. People write things in it with their finger, their names, the names of their loved ones, messages, as if trying to remember who they are. People have nothing to do here. They sit around all day and get sick in their minds. Then* ₁₅ *they get sick in their bodies.*

I live in RPC 2, which is also known as Bravo Camp. There are three compounds in this camp. RPC stands for "Regional Processing Centre". RPC 1 is where the people who work here live. They have their offices there. There is the medical facility ₂₀ *and our canteen.*

RPC 2 is where all the adult men live, men who tried to come to Australia on their own. RPC 3 is for families and children.

When I arrived in Nauru, no one believed me that I am seventeen. They said, "You have hair on your lip! You look like ₂₅ *a man!" I told them I had hair on my lip when I was fifteen, but they just shook their heads and put me in RPC 2 with all the other men. I told my case manager that I am seventeen, that I am a minor, but I couldn't prove it because I lost my documents at sea. There was nothing I could do.*

We live in large tents, dormitories with lines of beds. Most of the people who work here are from Nauru. The security person-nel are Australian. The doctors too. Some of them are nice to us, others call us by our ID number instead of using our names. We are nothing but numbers to them. Sometimes I think the nice 5 *guards are ashamed to be here.*

Every day the guards bring new rules into the camp. They tell us we have to do this, we have to do that, because these are the rules and you must obey the rules, but the rules keep chang-ing, and the changes make us feel angry. 10

They call this the "Pacific Solution", but I ask myself: where is the solution in this? I wanted to leave darkness for light, but now I find that I have left darkness for even more darkness.

*

I was completely out of breath by the time I got to the beach. I ran all the way, the strap of my bag digging into my shoul- 15 der, cutting my flesh. It hadn't felt that heavy when I left.

I kept wondering if Bashir would be there when I got there. What if he didn't trust me? What if he was scared I'd call the cops? Would he just leave? Disappear? Would he try to make it on his own? I had no idea what he thought, what 20 he wanted, or where he wanted to go. I didn't know if he had a plan at all.

The beach hut looked the same as it always did when I got there: its green paint flaking off the wooden planks due to the hot sun and sea air. There was no sign of life. Nothing 25 to show that someone was living there.

I knocked gently on the door. "Hi! Bashir! It's me, Cooper!" I waited a second before opening. "Bashir?"

No answer. I stepped inside. An unfamiliar smell stung my nostrils, a mix of wet clothes and food. It took my eyes a second to adjust to the darkness. The hut had no windows. I could see my sleeping bag on the floor. A half empty can of spam and a carton of milk stood next to it. Bashir's clothes were hanging from a line he'd put up, but Bashir was nowhere to be seen.

"Bashir?" I saw my watch on the floor. I picked it up and looked at the time. The hands had stopped at a quarter past ten.

I went outside. Above the sea, thin clouds stretched towards the horizon. The beach was empty. A few seagulls were flying above the mangrove trees.

I felt disappointed. It was just as I thought. Bashir had disappeared. He didn't trust me. He probably didn't trust anyone. But where had he gone? There was nowhere to go around Darwin.

I was just about to go back into the hut and start clearing up when I saw a shadow come out from the mangrove trees. It was Bashir. He was wearing my rugby sweatshirt and a pair of black shorts. His feet were bare. He was carrying one of Dad's fishing rods. A smile lit up his face.

"Hello, Cooper!" he said like we'd known each other all our lives, only to add in a less familiar way: "How do you do?"

How do you do?! I almost laughed. What book did he learn that from? Nobody speaks like that in Australia!

"Good, thanks. And you?"

"Me fine!" said Bashir, smiling like a champion. It was only then that I saw he was carrying a fish in his hand. Its wet scales sparkled in the light. He held it up proudly into the air and asked, "You hungry?"

6

Hope came back into my life today. My case manager told me I can move into RPC 3.

I packed my belongings into a plastic bag and followed one of the guards called Mister Stuart Thompson to my new living area. The tent where I am staying has air-conditioning. It is 5 *divided into small rooms. The walls are very thin, so you can hear everything your neighbour does, but it is a hundred times better than Bravo Camp. There we had no private space at all.*

I was sitting outside my tent this afternoon, watching the children playing in the sand, when a little girl came up to me. 10 *She had dark hair and eyes as black as night.*

"You look sad," she said to me in English. "Why are you so sad?"

I didn't know how to answer. What could I say? There are so many reasons to be sad here. I try to hide the sadness inside my 15 *heart, but this little girl, she saw it immediately.*

"I am not sad," I told her. "I am just alone."

"No, you are not alone," she answered. "I am with you."

Her logic made me smile.

"What is your name?" I asked. 20

"Saba. And yours?"

"Bashir."

Saba told me she came from Iran. She is in the camp with her parents and two brothers. One brother is the same age as me. The other is fourteen. Saba is ten years old, the same age as 25 *Amy. Saba and Amy are similar in many ways. They are both full of energy. They both like to laugh. They jump and sing and like to play games. But their lives couldn't be more different.*

"Me, I am never sad," Saba told me with a smile that warmed me like sunshine on a winter's day. "My father says we survived the sea, so we can survive anything."

I hope Saba is right.

5 *Sometimes I doubt it.*

*

Bashir knew how to prepare a fish even without the right equipment. He took the lid from the can of spam and used the edges like a knife. The fish's scales fell away like the petals of a sun-dried flower. When he was finished, he lit up Dad's

10 Primus stove, which he'd found at the back of the hut. Bashir used the empty can of spam as a frying pan, pressing the fish meat into small rectangles.

"How was your day?" I asked while Bashir cooked.

"Your day?" he replied.

15 I pointed at him. "No, *your* day. You. Here. Today. Everything okay?"

He nodded. "Everything okay."

"Nobody saw you?"

"Yes, yes!" He nodded enthusiastically. "Nobody see me."

20 He seemed much happier than the evening before. I asked him where he'd learned to fish.

"In Pakistan," he said. "In river. My father, he fish too."

There it was again: Pakistan. He'd mentioned it the day before, but he'd said he was from Afghanistan. It was time to

25 start piecing together the puzzle of Bashir's life.

"Why does your family live in Pakistan?"

"It long story."

"I've got time."

Bashir took a moment to empty the rectangle of fish onto the palm of his hand before turning it over to cook the other side.

"My family and me, we Hazara," he explained. "We live in Bamyan. The Taliban, they don't like Hazara. Hazara Shia 5 Muslim. Taliban Sunni. My family go from Afghanistan when I boy. We go Pakistan. We hope it good, but it no good."

He took the can off the stove and tipped the contents onto a plate.

"Eat," he said. 10

He picked up a piece of fish between his fingertips and put it in his mouth.

"Is good!" he exclaimed.

I followed his example. He was right. The fish was juicy and fresh and tasted slightly of spam. 15

"In Pakistan my family has many problems," Bashir continued while pressing the next portion into the hot can. "Many bombs in Pakistan. Not safe. Hazara people killed. My father killed. My family say I must go. I say: Where I go? They say England, Germany, Australia. I must find peace. I must 20 have future."

"Why Australia?"

He shrugged his shoulders. "People say Australia is nice country. Australia is peace. Democracy."

It is a nice country, I think. *In fact, it's a great country.* 25

And I want to show Bashir just how great it is.

"My family buys me ticket for plane. I fly from Karachi to Thailand. Fourteen people. Men and boys. Only three get past passport control. Others must go back to Pakistan. Me, I get past. I have phone. I have passport. I have telephone 30 number from man in Bangkok. This man, he help me. I call

him. We meet. He gives me new phone, new number. He says
we go Malaysia. Many weeks I wait in Thailand, then I go
with him to jungle. Other people, they come too. We cross
border. I wait one night in Malaysia, then we go to Indonesia."

"And from Indonesia you came here?"

"Yes. I have much fear. First time on boat. First time on
sea. I pray to Allah. I pray very hard. He help me."

"How old are you?"

"Seventeen."

Same age as me. For a moment I wonder what Bashir
would be like if he had been born in Australia.

"Do you know anyone here?" I asked.

Bashir's face lit up. "Yes!" he said, smiling. "I know you!"

7

*I saw Saba again today. She came out of her tent looking sick.
Her face was pale. Her eyes were like two black holes in her
skull.*

"What is wrong?" I asked.

She could not answer. She was too weak to speak.

*I took her to the medical facility. I pushed her to the front of
the queue. People shouted at me, but I ignored them. Saba was
so weak, she could hardly walk.*

*The doctor examined her and said, "She has an infection.
She must drink lots of water."*

*Always they say this to us when we are ill. Always they say
we must drink more water.*

"Can you give her some medicine?" I asked her. "She is only ten years old."

"We have no antibiotics here at the moment," the doctor said. "I am very sorry."

Always they say they are sorry. They say they are waiting for 5 *supplies from Australia, but we are so far away, the supplies do not come.*

When I first came here, I had a terrible toothache. My mouth was on fire. The pain was so bad, I stopped talking. Talking only caused more pain. I asked to see a dentist. The answer 10 *was: "There is only one dentist here. You have to wait." I waited nine days. Nine days of pain. When I finally saw the dentist he stopped the pain with an injection. I was so grateful, I almost cried for joy.*

It is not right the way they treat us here. We are not crimi- 15 *nals. We have done nothing wrong.*

*

Things went on like that for a couple of days, me visiting Bashir after school, bringing him food and clean clothes, fresh batteries for his torch. Every time I gave him something, he smiled, and every time he smiled, I wanted to give 20 him more.

Kate thought I was crazy, but that didn't stop her from asking me about him every day. Kate has a curious nature. The more I told her about him, the more she wanted to know. It didn't take long before she wanted to meet him personally. 25 I had the feeling that Bashir trusted me, so I asked him if I could bring her along.

"She like fish?" he asked.

I laughed. "Yeah, mate! She loves fish!"

Kate joined me on a Friday after school. When we got to the hut, we could smell the aroma of fried fish wafting through the mangrove forest. Fortunately, the wind nearly
5 always comes in off the sea, so the smell of Bashir's cooking never made it to the Surf Life Saving Club.

Bashir went all shy when I introduced him to Kate. He couldn't look her in the eye. He shook her hand and asked her to take a seat. He'd rolled up his sleeping bag into a cush-
10 ion and found a wooden crate for a table. He lit a candle. The hut almost felt homely.

Bashir proudly served the fish with crisps and pickles. We sat around the table, eating, and Kate soon started shooting questions at him. When Kate's older, she's going to have to be
15 a journalist. She always wants to understand things. Why? How? What then? She was asking Bashir questions faster than I could think of new ones.

"What's life like in Afghanistan? Did you go to school? What language do you speak? Can you read and write?
20 Where did you learn English? Do you have any brothers and sisters? Did your sister go to school in Afghanistan? Why did you move to Pakistan? What's it like there? What did your dad do for a living? Does your mum wear a burka? Is it true that most of the girls in Afghanistan get married before the
25 age of sixteen?"

Bashir answered each question with a patience I could only admire. It was interesting to hear what he had to say, but the story that stuck in my mind the most was the one about his father.

30 "One night men come to our house in Alamdar Road," he told us. "Taliban soldiers. They say my father is bad man.

They hit him. They kick him. They call him 'dog'. I see everything that night. I hide, but I see everything. I see them hit
my father with sticks, with their guns. They spit in his face. I
want to help, but I cannot. Too many men. I watch. I wait. I
hope they go away. I want to go to my father, but I know they ₅
will kill me."

He paused for a moment as if wondering if he had done
the right thing. Hide or help? Life or death? Was there a right
answer?

"Then bomb alarm goes off," he continued. "Every day ₁₀
bomb explodes in Pakistan. Sometimes Taliban. Sometimes
militants. Sometimes Pakistan army. Bombs everywhere.
The man who is boss tells his men to go outside. 'Go check,'
he says. The boss, he stays with my father. He takes out his
gun. He puts the gun to my father's head. I think he is going ₁₅
to kill him so I come out from my hiding and say: 'Stop!'"

Bashir was staring into the candle flame, the only source
of light in the hut. His face was old again. His eyes were full
of sadness, but he didn't cry.

"The man sees me. He points his gun at me. I think he kill ₂₀
me too. This is it. Life over. Short life. I see death in his eyes.
I am nothing to him. I am like dirt under shoe. Then bomb
explodes. Whole house shakes. Dust everywhere, like rain
from ceiling. I see nothing. I hear shouting. Women shouting. Men shouting. Children crying. The soldiers come back ₂₅
into house. I hear voices. They say, 'Hurry, boss, hurry! Come
with us!' Then I hear gunshot. I hear my father shout. Then
room goes silent. All is quiet. Dust stops falling from ceiling.
I see my father, white like ghost, covered with dust, lungs full
of blood, spitting red. I go to him. He smile, lips red. He put ₃₀

hand on my face. He says, 'I love you.' Then he dies in my arms. The man who did this, I will never forget them."

Kate didn't ask any more questions after that. We just sat there in silence, all three of us watching the candle's dancing
5 flame until Bashir spoke again.

"I am sad," he said, "but sadness cannot bring my father back. That is why I come here. Because I know next time, it is me who will die."

8

I watch people change in this camp. I see them when they come
10 *here. I see them forget who they are. They cannot sleep. They*
lose their appetite. They have no will. Their souls become empty.
They fall apart. I see it every day.

Saba does not understand what is happening to her family.
Every night she hears her mother cry. "Why is my mother cry-
15 *ing?" she asked me. "We came here for freedom. That is good, is*
it not, to be free? So why does my mother cry?"

Her father often gets angry. Yesterday he hit his youngest
son. The older son, the one who is only a few months older than
me, he gets into fights with other boys. The men in RPC 2, they
20 *fight all the time. They fight because they are angry. They fight*
like a protest. But this island is deaf. There is no one here to
listen to them. Children cry, parents shout, but no one can hear.

Today Saba asked me how long I have been here. For a
moment I thought about lying, but then I told her the truth:
25 *"Two months."*

"I will not survive here for two months," she said.

She has only been here for two weeks and already the light in her eyes is gone. There is no longer a smile on her face.

I told her she must be strong. "Remember what your father said. If you can survive the sea, you can survive anything."

She shook her head, like a leaf falling from a tree, and said, 5 *"I think my father was wrong."*

*

"What are we going to do?" Kate asked on the way home that evening, and the "we" in her question made me love her that little bit more.

I shrugged my shoulders. Whatever we did, it would be 10 wrong.

"He can't stay illegal forever, but to go to the cops now ..." Kate said. She looked up at the red evening sky. "It just doesn't feel right."

I agreed. The thought of Bashir being sent to a detention 15 centre made me feel ill. He hadn't come all this way to be locked up.

"We should teach him English," Kate suggested as we crossed the footbridge to Rapid Creek. "Make sure he's equipped to face the difficulties of daily life in Australia." 20

"We could get into trouble," I warned her.

"It's too late for that."

We didn't have a plan. The only thing we did have was time. As long as Bashir was with us, he couldn't be locked away. As long as he was with us, we could give him the best 25 start to his new life in Australia. We didn't want to let that chance pass.

Over the course of the next few days, we started to get organised. We brought pots and pans to the beach hut, bottles of drinking water. We gave Bashir a bowl to wash his dishes, towels to dry them. We drilled holes in the wall of
5 the hut so that Bashir could look out before leaving. It didn't matter if people saw him on the beach or in the woods, but we didn't want anybody seeing him going to and from the hut.

Kate and I became experts in secret operations. I took
10 Bashir's clothes home regularly and washed them. Kate persuaded her dad to clear out his wardrobe and get rid of all his old clothes. We gave Bashir a CD player and headphones and some batteries to power it. Kate had a bunch of audiobooks like "Harry Potter" and "Lord of the Rings". Bashir listened to
15 them around the clock. Kate borrowed a textbook on English grammar from the local library and photocopied the entire thing. Bashir did exercises during the day, and after school we came around to check his work like a couple of private tutors.

20 We told him everything he needed to know about Australia: about the cities and the land, about the education system and the job market, about our history and current affairs. It was a crash course in becoming Australian, and Kate and I were the best possible teachers. It made us realise
25 how much we loved our home. I even took my laptop along and showed Bashir some rugby matches. I explained Australian rules football to him. I didn't need to explain cricket. Bashir had already picked up the game in Pakistan.

At the same time Kate and I got in touch with a couple of
30 organisations we thought could help: The Refugee Council of Australia and another organisation to help unaccompanied

minors – children who had come without their parents. We wrote them emails under a false name. We thought it was better to be on the safe side. If they knew who we were, they could find Bashir. If they didn't, he was safe.

The replies that came all said the same: "Being illegal in Australia is not a long-term solution. We recommend that you go to your local authorities and find out what support is available." What else could they say? No one was going to encourage us to help an illegal immigrant.

For some reason Kate and I still didn't do what they suggested. We were convinced that we could help Bashir better than anyone else, even if he had to live in a hut for a while. At least he had a place of his own and two friends who cared about him. He kept the hut clean and tidy. He cooked and studied and went fishing every day. He soaked up everything we told him. It wasn't the best of lives, but there were worse.

Mum and Dad were happy to see me spending so much time with Kate. They thought she had a good influence on me. The only person who wasn't happy about the changes in my daily routine was Graham. He came up to me in school one day and said, "What's wrong? Is it something I said?"

Graham and I weren't close friends. We started hanging out just after Dad got into his campaign. Back then, Graham seemed like the right friend to have. He was into weed. It felt like the right thing to do. But Graham smoked every day, and that was not where I wanted to go. I don't know if he was really unhappy about losing me as a "friend" or if he just missed having his weed-buddy around, but I'd had enough of him.

"I'm just busy," I told him.

"Busy?" He said the word like he'd never heard it before. "Doing what?"

"A course down at the club. Life saving. Advanced."

He laughed. "Yeah? Who are you gonna save?"

5   I was starting to think Dad was right about Graham. Graham had a habit of knocking people. It gave him a kick to think people were stupid. It was starting to get on my nerves.

"Yeah, well, do whatever you want, superman," he said, "but don't come crying to me when you find out you don't

10 have a life."

Life could have gone on like that forever if things hadn't taken a dramatic turn a short time later. I was at the hut on a Friday afternoon, helping Bashir with some tricky English grammar, which even I couldn't explain, when suddenly the

15 door opened and my dad was standing there, a black silhouette against the bright sky. I don't know if he was squinting because it was dark inside or because he was surprised to see me, but it took him a while to speak.

"Coop?"

20 "Dad?"

Dad hadn't been to the hut for at least a year. His private life had stopped when his campaign to become Lord Mayor of Darwin started.

"Who is this?" he asked, looking at Bashir.

25 "Oh, yeah …" I said. Bashir and I exchanged a look. I could see the fear in his eyes. "This is a mate of mine."

Dad stepped into the hut, squinting at Bashir.

"Why is he wearing your clothes?"

I didn't have a good answer to that. Bashir was wearing

30 my old Australian cricket shirt, the one with my name on it, so it didn't make much sense to deny it. The pink Bermudas

were definitely not from me. They must have come from Kate's dad.

"What are you guys doing here?" Dad asked, his eyes scanning the books in front of us.

"We've got tests coming up," I explained. 5

"You didn't tell me you still came down here."

"Nor did you."

Usually that would have been enough to kick off an argument, but instead Dad chose to ignore it. He looked at Bashir, trying to place him. 10

"What's your name?"

Bashir glanced at me nervously. I gave him a nod.

"My name is Bashir," he said. Even his accent was starting to sound Australian.

"Bashir?" Dad repeated as if trying to solve a riddle. "Do 15 you go to school with Cooper?"

Again Bashir looked at me like a drowning swimmer. There was no way we were going to get out of this.

"No, Dad," I said. "He's from Afghanistan. He came here on a boat. I found him on the beach." 20

It was pretty blunt, I know, but there was no easy way to break it to him.

What followed was a silence like I've never heard before. It was deeper than the night, stiller than the windswept plains of the Outback. The fact that it was most probably going to 25 end in one almighty explosion made it all the harder to bear.

But the explosion didn't come. Dad didn't shout. He didn't throw up his hands and stamp his feet. He just looked at me, perfectly calm, and said, "We have to talk. Outside."

9

Saba came running into my tent today. She was crying.

"Take me away from here!" she said. "Put out my eyes!"

I took her in my arms and she cried into my shoulder until my T-shirt was wet with her tears.

5 *"My father's mind has left him," she said.*

"Why do you say this?" I asked. Her father is a good man, a clever man, a doctor.

Saba said I must go and see him for myself. After she calmed down, I left her in my tent and went to her family room. I found 10 *her father lying on his bed, his hand over his mouth, his shirt red with blood. His eyes were closed, but I could see from the movement of his chest that he was breathing.*

Saba's mother was sitting next to him, rocking to and fro, crying.

15 *"Water!" she said. "Get me water!"*

I ran to the bathroom and filled a bottle with water. Saba's mother took the water and washed away the blood from her husband's mouth, cleaning his face and neck. It was only then that I saw what he had done: Black thread criss-crossed his 20 *lips. His mouth was sewn up.*

I went to the doctor to inform her, but she said there was nothing she can do. She cannot force Saba's father to remove the thread. She cannot force him to speak or to eat. If this is what he wants, then nobody can change it. All she can do is 25 *disinfect the wounds and make sure there is no infection.*

Now I know that Saba was right. If her father does not die of madness, he will die of hunger.

*

"This is wrong."

It was the only thing Dad could say. He didn't just say it once or twice, he said it again and again, as if, by speaking the words, he could shape them into a different reality.

"This is wrong. This is wrong. This is wrong." 5

Dad's opinion didn't surprise me, but his calmness did. He paced up and down the beach, sending small clouds of sand into the air, his eyes scanning the ground as if hoping to find a solution to the problem there. I sat on the steps outside the hut, watching him, waiting, the door closed behind 10 me, knowing that Bashir was inside.

"This is wrong."

"Why?" I dared interrupt him.

Dad stopped in his tracks and looked at me in astonishment. "Because it's illegal, that's why." 15

"He's on his own, Dad. He was almost dead when I found him."

Dad's eyes flinched. What was that? Sympathy, or just plain fear?

He looked away before I could decide. 20

"That's not the point. I lock our front door every night not because I hate the people outside, but because I love the people inside. That's what borders are there for." He paused for a moment. "How long has he been here?"

"Five weeks." 25

"Jesus! Does he have any papers with him?"

"No."

"Passport?"

"He lost everything at sea."

"He was lucky." 30

"Lucky?"

"The boat he was on – he was the only one to survive."

Dad rubbed the back of his neck. "Do you trust him?"

"Totally."

"Does anybody else know about this?"

5   "Just Kate."

Dad nodded with some reassurance. "Good." He turned to me. "This can never come out, Coop, do you understand? If this comes out, I'm finished."

I felt a wave of disgust. For a moment I actually thought
10 Dad wanted to do the right thing here. I thought the problem was not me helping Bashir but about Bashir needing help. I was wrong. It wasn't. This was about him.

"Can't you think about someone else for a change?" I said.

"I am," he replied, raising his voice for the first time. "I'm
15 thinking about you, your mum, your sister. I'm thinking about our family and this city and all the things I'd like to do to make life here better. And yes, Coop, I'm thinking about Bashir too, because your little set-up here is not sustainable, is it? Or did you think you could go on like this forever?"

20   I didn't answer. That was the crazy thing about it. Kate and I knew it couldn't last. It took my dad to come along and put an end to it.

He turned away and looked out to sea. The waves were breaking gently onto the beach. The sky was darkening. Dad
25 took a deep breath and blew the air out of his lungs.

"You'd better back go in there," he said, nodding towards the hut. "We're leaving."

10

News of Saba's father spread through the camp like fire. Other men joined the protest, mainly from RPC 2. They sewed their lips together, refusing to eat or speak. Their friends said they would only stop their protest once they were heard, when someone finally listened to them. But who will see their protest? Who will hear what they have done? We have no telephones here. We have no internet. We cannot film these men and send their images out into the world. We cannot show the injustice we are suffering. We can only hope that the guards or the doctors or our case managers make this public, but their hands are tied. 10

There is one guard here who is nice to me. His name is Stuart Thompson. Mister Thompson is from Brisbane. He says hello to me when he sees me. He gives me a smile. I think he is a good man.

Today he came up to me and said, "Don't you do it." 15

I knew he was talking about the men who had sewn up their mouths.

"You have to try and understand our side of the story," he said. "Everybody here is here for a reason. I am sorry to have to say it, but it's true. If you break the law, there's a price to pay. I 20 *wish things were different, but they aren't. No one forced those men to do what they did. No one asked them to break the law. If they want to protest, that's fine, but it's not going to help them. I hope you understand that one day."*

Hope. There it was again, that word, like a distant echo 25 *growing quieter and quieter by the day.*

"I understand," I told him.

Now am I not so sure that Mister Thompson is a good man. If he was a good man then he wouldn't be here.

*

Dad was on the phone when Bashir and I came out of the hut. It sounded like he was talking to Mum. He hung up as soon as he saw us. He went up to Bashir and held out his hand.

5 "Hi. My name's Matthew Jackson. You can call me Matt if you want."

Dad didn't try to smile or be friendly. He just held out his big strong Australian hand and shook Bashir's.

"Nice to meet you, Mr Jackson," he said politely.

10 We followed Dad back to the car like strangers. He was parked near the university. Bashir didn't say a word the whole way. Something in his face had changed. That air of deep fatigue that had framed his eyes and shaped his smile when he'd first got here had returned. It made him look old 15 and helpless. It was sad to see it back so soon.

When I told him that we were going with my dad, Bashir panicked and grabbed the book of photocopies.

"I run," he'd said.

"No," I said. "Nobody's running. It's my dad we're talking 20 about here. We have to trust him. Everything will be fine."

I hoped I was right, but I didn't know for sure. Dad had a plan, I could tell that, I just didn't know what it was. I hoped his solution wasn't only good for us but good for Bashir as well.

25 "Where are we going?" I asked as we got into the car.

"Home."

"And then?"

Dad didn't answer.

"What will happen to Bashir?"

"He can stay with us for a while."

I couldn't believe what I was hearing.

"Yeah? How come?"

"It's better than sleeping in the hut, isn't it?"

"What's going to happen to him?"   5

Dad looked away. "Let's talk about that in the morning."

As dad pulled out of the parking lot, Bashir ducked.

"That's not necessary now," Dad told him, looking in the rear-view mirror. "You're with us."

Dad's calmness gave me the impression he had the situ- 10
ation under control. I wanted to thank him, tell him I was sorry about all the times we'd argued, about the things I'd said to him in the heat of the moment. I wanted to tell him he was a good man, a dad I was proud of, but something stopped me.   15

There must be a catch.

I decided not to ask any more questions. I let Dad drive and watched the green suburbs of Casuarina pass by. Rows of small houses, palm trees, petrol stations, the shopping mall, parks, all the way along Trower Road until we crossed 20
the bridge to Rapid Creek. This was the first time Bashir had seen Australia beyond the mangrove forest. I wondered what he made of it all.

Mum and Amy were waiting for us when we got home. They were standing on the porch, a reception committee 25
in matching colours. Mum looked a little uneasy. Amy was stroking Toohey's head. Toohey let out a deep growl when he saw Bashir.

"Toohey!" Amy pulled his collar. "Stop that!"

Toohey did as he was told, but Bashir still looked nervous. 30

"Welcome!" Mum greeted Bashir with a friendly smile, but the smile disappeared from her face when she turned to me. "And as for you, Cooper, that is the last time you lie to me!"

5 She was angry. Really angry.

Amy couldn't take her eyes off Bashir. She's ten and thinks older boys are princes from another planet. With his long black hair and high cheekbones, Bashir fitted her profile perfectly.

10 "Are you coming to live with us?" she asked.

Bashir didn't know what to say. He looked at me. I shrugged my shoulders. We both turned to Dad.

"Bashir just needs a place to stay for a few days," Dad explained. "Like Auntie Claire does when she comes from 15 Perth."

Amy's eyes widened in amazement. "Is Auntie Claire a refugee too?"

Dad laughed. "No! Your mum and Claire are as Australian as Vegemite!"

20 Mum pointed to the front door and led the way. "Why don't you come in?" she suggested. Amy grabbed Toohey's collar and dragged him up the steps. Bashir followed, watching Toohey cautiously. I stayed by the car, still trying to make sense of what was happening, and glanced at the fence. I 25 could see the roof of the porch next door.

"What if someone sees him?" I asked.

"We say he's the son of a mate of mine from Melbourne," Dad answered and opened the boot.

"When are you going to tell the authorities?"

30 Dad snorted and slammed the car door shut. "Give me a break, Coop! I *am* the authorities!"

He walked straight past me and up the steps.

"I'm going to sort this out," he said. "And no one's gonna get hurt."

11

Saba went to school for the first time today. The Australian government made a deal with the Republic of Nauru to let children from the camp attend a nearby primary school. They are calling it a "pilot project" – a test to see how things work. Ten children were selected. Saba was one of them, probably because her English is so good. Saba told me she was a very good pupil in Iran.

Saba was so excited about going to school again. "This is the beginning of a new life," she said as we waited for the bus by the gates. "Soon they will let us out of here. Soon we will go to Australia and I will study and go to university one day."

I saw that light in her eyes – the same light I saw when I first met her. I thought I would never see that light again.

Hope was back.

I was excited for Saba too. All day I waited for her to return. What would she think of school? What stories would she tell about her day? What games would she play at break? What subjects would she learn? Maybe she had even made a friend. I felt like a part of me was going to school with her.

At the end of the day, I waited at the gates for the bus to return. It came along the road in a cloud of dust. The bus doors opened. I was expecting to see Saba jump off with a big smile on her face. Instead she came down the steps holding her schoolbag against her chest, her head bowed.

"What is it?" I asked as the guards brought her back into the camp. "What happened?"

Saba's eyes filled with tears.

"I never want to go back there again!" she cried. "The teach-
5 *ers do not want us there. The children hate us. We had to sit at the back of the class all day. Nobody spoke to us. At break the children said we are dirty and smelly. They said we will make them sick. They told us to stay in the camp where we belong. If that is what they want, then that is what I will do! I will never go*
10 *back there again. Never! I will stay here for the rest of my life!"*

*

Dad called a family meeting in the morning. He told me to ask Kate over. She already knew what had happened. I'd spoken to her the night before.

"I'll be there in twenty minutes," she said.

15 The doorbell rang after ten.

We met up in the lounge. Dad carried in a tray of soft drinks and biscuits, more as something to preoccupy us than because we were hungry. Bashir had eaten enough breakfast to feed half a rugby team. Amy nibbled at a biscuit, but only
20 because she didn't understand what was going on. The rest of us were too tense to eat. Toohey sat at Amy's feet, waiting to pick up some crumbs from the least careful member of our family.

Kate seemed kind of embarrassed about being there. My
25 parents knew she'd lied, and for some reason a lie from Kate was much worse than a lie from me. She felt guilty about it, but it was too late to have regrets. Our secret was out. We had to deal with it now as best we could.

"So tell us your plan," said Mum, leaning back in the armchair as if Dad were about to start telling a story.

Dad sat on the edge of the sofa, his fingertips touching. He took a moment to focus before beginning to speak: "I think I have an idea how we can get you both out of this," he said, looking at me and Kate. "Sooner or later, Bashir is going to have to enter the system. That's something we all have to accept. However, I would like to avoid going to the authorities straightaway for various reasons. No refugee boats have arrived in Darwin since Bashir's boat. If Bashir goes to the police now, they're going to put two and two together and ask him where he's been for the last five weeks."

"I can say I was alone," Bashir interrupted.

Dad gave a short, disdainful laugh and shook his head. "You underestimate the Australian Police Force, my friend. They'll ask you so many questions, you won't know if you're coming or going. Sooner or later they'll find a hole in your story and rip you apart. After that, it won't take them long to trace everything back to Cooper and Kate, then to us. That's what you get for trying to help illegal immigrants in this country."

Mum tried to force a smile. Dad paused and took a deep breath.

"We have to face the facts. You've broken the law. If the police find out what you did, they'll either press charges or give you a caution. If they press charges and you are found guilty, you'll both have a criminal record. No university in the country will touch you. No serious employer will give you a job. You could even have problems travelling abroad."

Kate bowed her head in shame. Bashir closed his eyes as if the burden of what had happened lay on his shoulders.

"So what are you suggesting?" I asked.

"My idea is simple. Bashir has to come to Austra
ond time."

Bashir looked up, first to Dad, then to me. I had no idea
5 what he was talking about.

"The boat Bashir was on is not going to be the last," Dad
continued. "Others will follow. And when the next boat
comes, Bashir will be on it."

Bashir frowned. "I don't understand. How will I get on the
10 boat?"

"That's the beauty of it. You won't have to. I've spoken to
the coast guard. As soon as the next boat comes, they'll let
me know. Then we go down to the beach, first thing in the
morning or late at night, when the place is deserted, and you
15 arrive for a second time. You put on your old clothes. You go
into the water. You come out. Cooper and I find you. We call
the police. They pick you up. You tell them you were on the
boat and fell overboard. They'll take you to hospital and give
you a medical check. The police will question you. You'll be
20 registered. You can claim asylum through the normal chan-
nels."

Dad paused and looked into our faces. I don't know if he
was expecting triumphant cries or a pat on the back, but I
could hardly believe what I was hearing.

25 "What about the other people on the boat?" Bashir asked.
"What if the police ask them questions about me?"

"Asylum seekers stick together," Dad assured him. "No
one will betray you."

I stood up. "This is bullshit!" I told Dad. "Bashir came to
30 Australia for help. Is this your idea of helping him?"

Dad looked at me sternly. "There's an immigration centre here in Darwin. There are Afghans there. I'll make sure he goes there."

"Why can't he stay with us?" asked Amy as if she had completely missed the point. 5

"Because it's the law," Dad replied and looked at the biscuits on the coffee table.

"You can change the law," Amy said. "You're the Mayor."

Dad tried to laugh, but his laughter stuck in his throat.

I turned to Kate. Her face was buried in her hands. 10

"Kate, we can't let this happen."

She looked up and shook her head, tears in her eyes. "I'm sorry."

I thought I was going to start crying myself for a moment. My throat had gone dry. I wanted to shout, I wanted to 15 scream. Something had to happen.

Bashir stood up. "It's okay, Cooper," he said, his hand on my arm. "Your father is right. This is the only way."

12

Today a politician from the Department of Immigration and Border Protection came to see us. He was a tall man in a black 20 *suit with grey hair and glasses. He walked around the camp with a group of guards and other men in suits, sweating. He inspected the tents, he inspected the toilets. He ate the food from the canteen.*

The guards told us beforehand, "You have to be on your best 25 *behaviour today! Don't even think about making trouble!"*

As if we would cause trouble! The guards are the ones with sticks and guns. We do not want to fight. We came here to get away from fighting.

People here were full of hope about his visit. A real politician
5 *was coming to see us! A man who can make decisions. A man who can listen. Of course we are going to be nice to him! We are not going to shout at him and make him think that we are bad people. We are going to smile and say, "Maybe you can do this for us. Maybe you can do that." We will not turn him away.*

10 *At midday, all the refugees gathered outside under the hot sun. The air was wet with humidity. The man from the Department of Immigration was given a microphone. He wiped the sweat from his forehead and spoke into the microphone. He did not say hello. He did not tell us he would help us. He just said,*
15 *"I am here to tell you that we will try our best to keep you out of our country, because you are the people who came by the window. You didn't use the door, you came by the window, and you don't deserve to stay here. We will use any method to get you out."*

20 *Then he put down the microphone and the guards surrounded him and walked him out of the gates.*

That was it. No help, no listening, just the message: "You will never come to Australia." That was his promise.

This man, he slapped us in the face today and all we can do
25 *is fall to our knees.*

*

For the next couple of days, Bashir settled into his new life in our home. He slept in my room, took his first bath in God knows how long, and continued to study during the day.

He ate with us every evening, watched TV with us, played cricket with my sister in the garden. He even started to relax around Toohey. It was funny that Bashir was scared of him. The only thing Toohey was capable of harming was himself. He'd once found a tub of ice cream in the kitchen and had eaten it so quickly that he spent the next 24 hours vomiting.

Amy and I stopped having friends over, which wasn't a problem. Amy enjoyed inventing lies to invite herself over to her friends. "Mum's not feeling well" or "My brother's having a party" or "Dad needs some space". Kate was the only friend of mine who came over to our house. Dad told her not to say anything to her parents about Bashir, and she didn't need to be reminded.

Dad was busy in the lead-up to the election. The highlight of the campaign was a TV debate between him and his opponent, scheduled for the week before the election. He left the house early every morning and came home late at night. Some days, the only time we saw him was on the local news.

At first, Mum was reserved around Bashir. She clearly didn't feel comfortable, not because she had a problem with where Bashir came from, but because she hated the idea of doing something wrong. Her dad was a lawyer. Her mum was a lawyer. Her whole life had been about right and wrong. Bashir could sense her discomfort and kept his distance, which only made things worse.

When he wasn't around, Mum commented on Bashir's behaviour. He had no table manners, she said. He slurped when he drank his tea. He ate with his mouth open. "Have you seen the shower after he's used it?" I heard her tell Dad one day. "There are little black hairs all over the place! He never washes it down."

Bashir didn't just eat differently, he smelled different too. And to make things worse, he squeezed the toothpaste from the top of the tube, not from the bottom. That was near to criminal in Mum's book. "It's so wasteful!" she claimed.

5 Every time I heard her complain, I thought about telling Bashir, but I decided not to. I didn't want him to feel under pressure. I decided not to. Instead I reshaped the toothpaste after he'd used it, and washed down the shower once he'd left the bathroom, and made sure I always had plenty to talk
10 about at dinner so that Mum was listening to me and not watching Bashir's table manners.

At the end of his second week, Bashir came into the kitchen when my sister and I were getting ready for school. He was dressed and looked more awake than I was. Dad had
15 already left. Mum was having a quick breakfast with us. She's a manager at Darwin's convention centre and she always drops Amy off at school on her way to work.

"Morning, Bashir!" she said when she saw him. "Would you like something to eat?"

20 "No, thank you kindly." Bashir had a great way of being polite. It disarmed you entirely. "I just wanted to ask if you would mind if I pray?"

Mum looked surprised. "I'm sorry?"

"Today is Friday," Bashir said. "I pray on Friday. I wanted
25 to ask if this okay for you?"

Mum looked baffled. "Yeah. Sure," she said.

"May I use the living room?" The morning sun was shining through the bay windows, filling the room with light.

"Feel free."

30 Amy stopped eating her breakfast and followed Bashir into the living room. She didn't ask if she could join him.

She just sat down on the sofa and watched him until Toohey came in and lay down at her feet.

Bashir prayed out loud. I tried to ignore him, but my curiosity got the better of me, so once I finished my breakfast, I got up and followed Amy next door. 5

Bashir was standing in the middle of the room, looking out of the window. His hands hung by his side as he prayed. I heard the name "Mohammad" and the words "Allahu Akabar", but that was all I understood.

After raising the palms of his hands into the air, he 10 dropped to his knees and moved his body forward until his forehead touched the carpet. In this position, he continued to say his verses, his face to the ground, before sitting back and placing his hands on his knees. The sun shone on his back and cast a long shadow over the carpet. He repeated 15 this action twice before standing up again and bringing his hands together.

It took me a while before I realised that Mum was standing next to me, watching Bashir as well.

"I'm gonna miss him, you know," she said in a whisper. 20 "It's a real shame he has to go."

13

The camp burned last night. I was lying in bed when I heard men shouting. "Nauru Guantanamo! Nauru Guantanamo!" they chanted. This is what some people call it here.

The voices grew louder and louder. I went outside to see 25 *what was going on. There were buildings on fire. Tents were burning in RPC 2. The guards stood outside, armed with riot gear. The men broke down the fences, picking up stones and pieces of metal, and disappeared into the night. The guards could not stop them. There were too many of them.*

I thought of the protests I saw in Pakistan. There were often demonstrations on the streets of Quetta. Every demonstration began with chanting and ended in violence. There was tear gas. There were bullets. There were dead bodies in the street.

"Nauru Guantanamo! Nauru Guantanamo!"

Why do the men do this? They will achieve nothing. What is the point in escaping? There is nowhere to go. You cannot leave this island.

This morning smoke still rose from the remains of Bravo camp. They say there was much fighting on the island last night. When news spread that refugees had escaped, the locals joined in the search. They didn't want foreigners roaming their island.

When the man from the Department of Immigration was here, we hoped for improvements. Now things will only get worse. That is what comes of violence. Why are we so stupid to think it could achieve anything? Why does this happen again and again? Where will all the men from RPC 2 sleep now? Everything is destroyed. And for what? Life will only become more difficult.

*

Bashir was smart. He knew that Mum was the key to our family, and he wanted her on his side. She came home one day to find that he'd emptied the dishwasher. Not only that, he'd even found the right place for all the dishes – something that Dad and I only seldom achieved. Mum was delighted. The next day she came home to find that Bashir had taken down the washing and folded it into neat piles. But it was going too far when he started ironing Dad's shirts.

"That's not necessary," Mum told him, although everybody knew she hated ironing. Normally Dad did the ironing in front of the TV, but due to his election campaign, Mum 5 had started doing some of his household duties, including ironing, which she really loathed.

"Please, Mrs Jackson," Bashir said, "you help me, I help you, if that's okay with you."

In the end, Mum gave in, though perhaps not as reluc- 10 tantly as she liked to think.

Around the same time, I began to notice that the shower was always clean after Bashir used it. He left the toothpaste just the way Mum liked it. His table manners became strikingly good. He never once slurped when he drank his tea. 15 Mum had no reason to complain any more.

One day Bashir discovered a box of my old Lego in the cupboard where Dad kept the ironing board. He asked me if he could use it and, though surprised he should be interested in playing with kids' toys, I agreed. 20

He started making buildings, not like a kid, but like someone who was trying to understand the nature of what he was constructing. He found pictures of famous landmarks, like the Sydney Opera House, and tried to build them. He built Parliament House, the Shine Dome, skyscrapers from Aus- 25 tralia Square. As soon as he had built one, he demolished it and began another. It seemed there was nothing he couldn't build.

Dad was impressed. Bashir said he wanted to become an engineer and I could see why. Dad could hardly contain his 30 enthusiasm. He'd always wanted to me to become an engineer, but it wasn't going to happen. Architecture just wasn't me.

Bashir brought something magical into our house. Everybody liked him. Mum liked him because he was polite and helpful; Dad liked him because he was hard-working and smart; Amy adored him because he played with her. Even Toohey loved having someone around the house all day instead of being at home on his own. And I liked him because we were similar and yet different in so many ways.

But when Graham Barton turned up at our front door one day, I realised that our family harmony was more than fragile.

"You wanna hang out?" he asked as he hovered on our front doorstep. I didn't let him into the house.

"Na. I'm revising."

Graham snorted his disapproval. He took a bag of weed out of his pocket and flashed it at me. "I've got some good stuff."

"Are you crazy?" I glanced over my shoulder. "My mum's at home!"

"Come on, mate! We haven't had a smoke in ages! Let's go to the park. It's Saturday!"

"I don't want a smoke, thanks."

"Don't ignore me like this, man! What have I done? You don't even talk to me any more."

"I've got things on my mind."

"Yeah? Well so have I. Isn't that what friends are for? Someone to talk to."

I didn't say anything to that. I don't remember ever having done much talking with Graham.

"Can I come in for drink?" he asked.

Bashir was in the back garden playing with Amy. Mum was up in the office. I just wanted him to go.

"What? You won't even let me into your house?" Graham said. "What is wrong with you, man? I'm not a bloody leper!"

I decided that not letting him might arouse more suspi- 5 cion than telling him to leave, so I stepped back and invited him in. It didn't really matter if he saw Bashir. We had an explanation. Now was the time to use it.

Graham followed me into the kitchen. I gave him a soft drink. It didn't take long for him to spot Bashir out in the 10 garden.

"Who's that?" he asked.

"His dad is a friend of my dad's. He's from Melbourne."

"Yeah? Looks more Chinese to me."

"His parents are from Afghanistan," I said, a little too 15 quickly.

"Refugee?"

"No, mate. Second generation."

Graham laughed. "Well, we're all immigrants, aren't we?"

He finished his drink. I didn't offer him another one. 20

"You can keep this if you want," he said and took the bag out of his pocket.

"No way, man! Put it away!"

I grabbed the bag and pressed it back into Graham's hand.

"Come on, Coop! Just relax! You can smoke it after the 25 exams."

"I already said: I don't want it!"

"What is wrong with you, man?"

"There's nothing wrong with me!"

The front door opened. Graham and I froze. I heard Mum's 30 footsteps upstairs.

"Hi!" she called.

I pushed the bag back into Graham's hands, more forcefully this time. "Put it away!"

Graham turned and dropped the bag. The kitchen door opened. Dad looked in.

"Oh, Coop! You're here," he said.

"Hi, Dad."

Graham swooped down to pick up the bag.

"Graham," said Dad. His one-word-greeting. Always a conversation-killer.

"Afternoon, Mr Jackson!" said Graham as he slipped the bag back into his pocket. Dad hesitated for a moment and looked at us suspiciously. I took a sniff to make sure the air didn't smell of grass.

"Graham was just leaving," I said.

"Yeah. Right. Goodbye, Mr Jackson."

I pushed Graham out into the hall. Dad went upstairs. I followed Graham to the front door and waited until I heard Dad talking to Mum.

"Don't ever come here again, okay?" I told him. "I don't want your weed. And I don't want your friendship."

I slammed the door, leaving Graham looking speechless on the porch. I think he got the message

14

Saba's asylum application was accepted today. Her family has been granted a Temporary Protection Visa. Saba will leave the camp soon. Her family will go and live in Papua New Guinea. Saba doesn't understand this. Her boat landed on Christmas

Island, and Christmas Island belongs to Australia. That is where her family wanted to go, so that is where her family applied for asylum. But Australia will not have them.

"Papua New Guinea is a free country," her family's case manager told them. "You will be safe there." 5

Saba is more scared of living in Papua New Guinea than staying in the camp. She knows nothing about the place. "Can you study in Papua New Guinea?" she asked me. "Do they have jobs for my father? Do the people like strangers?"

I could not give her an answer. 10

Her father went to the medical facility this morning and had the thread removed from his mouth. He ate his first meal in almost a week. He vomited straightaway. The doctors put an ointment on the wounds around his mouth and gave him medicine to calm his stomach. He signed the papers and shook 15 *hands with his case manager.*

My case manager told me I will probably be on Nauru for another five to eight months. "Things would be easier if you were here with your family," she said. "Families have priority. But young men on their own – they have to wait." 20

She saw the tears in my eyes. "I am very sorry," she said. "You are a victim of the policy to stop the boats."

How cruel it is to say these things to people who have left their homes and experienced so many difficulties to get here, just to find peace and freedom. Where is hope now? Where is 25 *freedom? Do they not understand? I wouldn't be here if I didn't have to be.*

*

Australian politics is a simple business. Effectively there are two parties: the Labor Party and the Liberal Party. People grow up with an allegiance to either one or the other. It's a family thing. If your parents are Labor, you're more likely to ₅ be Labor too. If your grandparents were Liberal, you'll probably be Liberal as well. There's not a lot of fluctuation.

My dad is a member of the Liberal party, the more conservative arm of Australian politics. The Liberal Party stands for traditional values, minimum state interference, individ-
₁₀ ual choice, and business. It was a Liberal government that introduced the "stop the boats" policy, although their predecessors, the Labor Party, didn't exactly welcome illegal maritime arrivals either. They were the ones who reopened the offshore detention camps.

₁₅ Dad wanted to become Lord Mayor of Darwin because he believed that business opportunities in Darwin were much bigger than anyone realised.

"I have three words," he liked to say. "China, China, and China."

₂₀ He was a businessman, not a politician. He promised to improve all public services as a result of increased trade with China. That was his only political idea. He wanted to expand the harbour, improve relations with our trading partners and make Darwin Australia's gateway to Asia. He had plans.
₂₅ Big plans.

As the final TV debate drew closer, Dad grew more and more nervous. It was a *live* show, to be broadcast on Darwin's local TV channel and streamed on the Internet. On the day of the debate itself, it was hardly possible to talk to Dad at
₃₀ all. Whatever I did was wrong. If I said something, he told me to be quiet. If I was quiet, he asked me what the matter was.

When Amy laughed, he said she was silly. If she asked him a question, he told her to stop being so demanding. It went on like that all day.

To be fair, we were all pretty nervous. The families of the two main candidates had been invited to appear on the show as well. We were meant to sit on stage as part of the background. We didn't have to say anything, thank God, but it was still pretty nerve-wracking.

Mum, Amy and I sat on a blue sofa – the colour of the Liberal Party – while our Labor counterparts sat on a red one. Dad and his opponent stood in front of us, facing the studio lights and the audience, while three interviewers sat at the front of the stage. They asked a selection of questions chosen from members of the audience and the wider public. The candidates had a minute in which to answer each question.

"What is your position on Carbon Tax?"

"How can Child Care Services be improved?"

"What should Darwin do about its asylum seekers?"

I thought of Bashir following the TV debate at home. I bet they didn't have shows like this in Afghanistan.

Dad didn't come up with any surprising answers. There was nothing controversial about his opinion. He supported government policies but stressed the need to meet "these people" with humanity. Whatever the subject, Dad always came back to his core message: *Make me mayor and I will boost business in Darwin. With business booming there'll be enough jobs for everyone – including the immigrants.* People, he said, were not the problem. It was their method of coming here illegally which made it an issue. I didn't quite see how he could separate the two. If you're desperate to leave your country, you'll do anything, won't you?

The debate was just coming to a close when there was a scuffle at the back of the studio. The stage lights blinded me, so I couldn't see anything at first. I heard someone shouting. Dad stopped talking mid-sentence. The interviewers spun
5 around on their seats to see what the disturbance was about. A shadow emerged from the darkness. It was Graham's dad.

Dad took a step towards him. "Mr Barton?" he said, unable to hide his astonishment. "Is everything all right?"

Graham's dad looked terrible. His hair was a mess. His
10 eyes were red. He was crying.

"Bullshit, that's what this is!" he shouted, waving in Dad's direction. "Don't you listen to him! Nothing he says is true!" He pointed shakily at Dad.

Dad remained amazingly calm. "Mr Barton, what are you
15 doing here?"

"He's a liar, that's what he is!" Mr Barton's speech was slurred. He was drunk. "He's a goddam liar!"

I had no idea what Graham's dad was talking about. Mr Barton and my dad hardly knew each other. I was surprised
20 my dad even recognised him.

"Mr Barton, please ..." Dad squatted down at the edge of the stage in a thwarted attempt to see eye to eye. "What are you doing here?"

"You see this man?" Barton continued, turning to the
25 audience and pointing at Dad. "He sits here with his wife and kids, looking all smart and clever, Mister I-know-it-all, but I bet his wife doesn't know what he gets up to when she's not around!"

Barton paused. The entire room was humming with
30 silence. Everybody wanted to know.

"What about you, Mrs Jackson?" Barton turned to my mother. "Do you know what he gets up to?"

Dad threw Mum a helpless glance. She barely managed to shake her head.

"Well, allow me to enlighten you." Mr Barton laughed. 5 "Your husband, Mrs Jackson, is a cheat, that's what he is! A goddam cheat! And do you know how I know? 'Cos he cheated with MY WIFE!"

As Barton spat the words out, he lost his balance and almost collapsed before two security guards arrived out of 10 nowhere and grabbed him.

"You ask him, Mrs Jackson!" Barton screamed as the security guards dragged him away. "You ask him what he was doing with my wife!"

The rest of his cries could hardly be heard, but it was too 15 late. Everybody had heard what he'd said.

Dad remained still at the edge of the stage as if turned to stone. All eyes were on him. After what seemed like an eternity, he slowly stood up and turned towards us on the velvety, blue sofa. 20

The sorrow in Dad's eyes ripped my heart apart. I heard Mum swallow next to me. I saw the tears swell up in her eyes. Her face hardened as she fought the tears back. Before she could control them no longer, she stood up and walked silently out of the studio, her head held high. 25

15

Saba's family left the camp today. The guards gave them two plastic bags to pack their belongings. They came with nothing. They left with nothing. Just a few clothes more.

I went to the gate to wish them goodbye.

5 *"I will miss you," Saba told me.*

"I will miss you too."

"You must be strong", she said. "Remember, you survived the sea ..."

"... so I can survive anything."

10 *Saba smiled.*

"I will think of you always," I told her. "Your memory will give me strength. Good luck!"

This little girl with her brilliant bright eyes, who had left her home months ago, was the strongest person I knew.

15 *"I want you to have this," she said and pressed something into my hand. She closed my fingers around it, wrapping it into the palm of my hand. "Don't open it until I am gone."*

I thanked her. Her mother came and took her hand. I watched as the guards escorted her family out of the gates and

20 *onto a waiting bus. In a few hours they would be landing in Papua New Guinea to begin a new life.*

Only after the bus had disappeared did I open my hand to look at the gift Saba had given me. It was small butterfly made of cans, the wings brightly coloured with Coca-Cola and

25 *Fanta. It was fine and intricate, made with love and care. The wings were broad and light. It almost looked like it could fly. I raised my hand into the air and sent it flying into the air. For a moment, the butterfly caught a breeze and rose higher before turning around and falling lifelessly to the ground.*

*

Mum and Dad are no angels. They've had their rows before, but the mood at home had never been as bad as this. The strange thing was, they didn't even argue. There was no shouting or door slamming, no raised voices or accusations. Dad said that Mr Barton had lied, that the story was different. We overheard him explaining to Mum, but we didn't want to know the details.

"I didn't cheat on you," he promised. "I didn't have an affair."

I think Mum believed him, but it made no difference. The public humiliation couldn't have been worse. "I'm going to my sister's for a couple of days," she told us. "I just need some space."

She told us not to worry, that everything would be okay, that they would fix whatever had been broken. Dad tried to persuade her to stay, but she refused quietly and took the next flight west.

After Mum had left, Dad sat down with me and told me his side of the story. Something *had* happened between him and Graham's mum, just not what Mr Barton said. Dad had been at some fundraising event down at the wharf. Graham's mum had been there too. They'd both been drinking. They'd shared a taxi home at the end of the evening. Dad dropped Mrs Barton off at her house. He was going to walk home from there, but before leaving, he kissed her goodbye, a kiss meant for her cheek which had landed too close to her lips. Dad felt bad about it, but that was all that had happened. He hadn't seen Mrs Barton since.

Mr Barton had been away at the time. Graham or his brother must have seen what happened. One of them probably told their dad.

"So tell that to the press," I said.

5 "It's too late for that," Dad said. "People believe what they see, not what they hear. First rule of politics. You see a husband on TV accusing another man of cheating with his wife, it doesn't matter what you say. You can protest until you're blue in the face, no one's going to believe you. And even if
10 Barton didn't tell the truth, I not exactly innocent, am I?"

Dad announced his withdrawal from the election the following day. "I made a mistake, and before I can make good on that, I have to make good with my family," he told the press. He cancelled all his appointments. He wrote Mum a long let-
15 ter telling her that he loved her and that he wanted her back. He called her again and again, but the only person he spoke to was Auntie Claire. He wanted fly to Perth to spend some time with Mum. He asked us if that would be okay. Normally I would have jumped at the opportunity, but there was one
20 thing Dad had forgotten: "What about Bashir?"

Dad sighed. "I'm more worried about your mum right now."

"What if a boat comes while you're away?"

"It's a risk we're going to have to take."

25 When Dad finally did manage to speak to Mum, she agreed to meet him, but asked him to give her a few more days. I was happy they were talking again.

Dad booked his flight and waited for his trip with growing impatience. He spent his days with Bashir. They watched
30 sport together, worked out in the basement together, cooked and ate together. Bashir knew how to cook, so he taught Dad

some Afghan dishes. One was called *Qabuli*, rice with raisins, carrots and lamb, with pistachios on top. They made *Kofta* together, spicy meatballs, and a stew called *Korma*. Dad really got into it. While they cooked, Dad told Bashir about Australian politics, how the state machine worked, and why it was the way it was. Every afternoon when I came home from school, they were either watching Australian Rules Football or playing chess.

"Bashir's a natural!" Dad praised him. "He's only been learning a week and he can already beat me! What d'you say to that, Coop?"

I'd say that is somebody we should want to have *in* our country, not someone we should turn away.

The night before his flight to Perth, Dad was in the best of moods. He was nervous and excited at the same time, and happier than I've seen him for years. It made me think of the saying "sometimes you have to lose everything in order to gain yourself ".

We ordered pizza and sat down in front of the box for a TV dinner. We'd only just started eating when Dad's phone rang. He checked the number, frowned and answered. He was on his feet in a second. He grabbed the remote and pressed the mute button. Something was wrong.

My first thought was: *Something's happened to Mum!* But Dad wasn't upset in a bad way. He was just focussed.

After a while Dad thanked the caller and hung up. He looked at Bashir and I could see in his eyes that this was the moment we'd all been waiting for.

"It's time," he said.

He didn't need to say more. We knew exactly what he was talking about.

"Go and get changed!" Amy squealed.

Dad told everyone to relax. There was no hurry, he said. It was too early to go down to the beach. We had to make sure we were on our own. Bashir couldn't be seen before going
5 into the water. He said we should wait until the football game was over.

We sat there for another hour, watching the ball being passed around the field, nobody saying anything. The pizza remained untouched. At around 9 o'clock we went outside
10 to the car. It was a moonless night. A light wind ruffled the trees. We drove over to Casuarina in silence. The air was charged with anticipation and fear. We parked close to the club and went down to the beach with Toohey.

Everyone thinks the sun always shines in Darwin. It does
15 most of the time, but every year we also have a rainy season. We have some major thunderstorms, and when it rains, believe me, it pours. When we got to the beach that evening, you could feel a storm coming in the air. The wind whipped our faces. The sand stung our eyes. The waves roared like
20 angry giants. No boats would be out tonight.

I looked up and down the beach. There wasn't a soul to be seen.

"Are you ready?" Dad asked Bashir.

Bashir nodded.

25 "Make sure you get your hair wet," Dad reminded him. "And don't go in too far. We don't want to lose you."

Bashir nodded again. "Thank you, Mr Jackson," he said. "Thank you for everything."

He looked at us one last time before walking into the sea.

PART TWO

1

*I wish I could say that I am dreaming, but I am not. I wish
I could say that my mind is deranged by a violent fever, that
what I saw today was no more than a hallucination, a cruel
trick of this hot and humid island, but I cannot. I wish, I wish,*
5 *but I know that it is not true. What I saw today was real.*

*He is here. In this camp. The man who killed my father. He
is here, locked up between the same fences as I am, watched by
the same guards as I, banished to this remote island.*

I was on my way to the canteen today when I saw him. He
10 *was sitting outside one of the tents in Bravo, smoking a cigarette. He had no beard, but I remembered the scar on his forehead, his black bitter eyes, the sound of his voice. I hid behind
a tent and watched him. I could not take my eyes off him. I had
to know I was not dreaming.*

15 *When the man finished his cigarette, he stood up and
walked over to the canteen. It was then that any doubt left me.
The way he held his right leg, his knee stiff, was the final confirmation. It was with that walk that he left my father dead.*

What is he doing here, this Taliban fighter, this monster of
20 *war? He is not a refugee. He is not a victim. He cannot claim
asylum. Why is he here?*

*I went back to my tent, my mind dizzy with fear. This man,
he knows my face. He saw me as he stood over my father. He
would have killed me, too, if he'd have had the chance, but the*
25 *bomb stopped him.*

*Would he recognise me today? More than a year later?
Would he see the fear in my eyes? I am the only person in this*

*camp who knows who he is. I am the only person who can
betray him. If he sees me, I will never leave this place alive.*

*

Darwin was named after Charles Darwin, the British nat-
uralist who came up with the theory of evolution. Charles
Darwin spent a lot of time on boats, sailing around the 5
world, studying birds and other animals, from England to
South America and Australia. He never actually set foot in
what would later become the city of Darwin, but the ship he
travelled on came here a few years after his first voyage, and
the captain decided to name the natural harbour after him. 10

Charles Darwin never used the phrase "survival of the fit-
test". He never saw life as a competition between the species. He was interested in the way plants and animals were
able to adapt to their environment and how that process
changed them physically over millions of years. He said that 15
humans are the most advanced species on earth because of
their brain. Sometimes I ask myself if that's a good thing.

I will never forget the sight of Bashir coming out of the
sea that night, his clothes wet and torn, looking lost and
scared. Dad had already made the call. We heard the siren 20
screaming in the distance, saw the flashing light through
the mangrove trees. The next thing I knew, two policemen, a
man and a woman, were hurrying down the beach towards
us, their torches cutting the darkness. The policewoman recognised Dad. The policeman asked Bashir if he could speak 25
English. Bashir said yes but kept his answers short so that
his excellent spoken English didn't betray him. The police-

woman took down Dad's account of what had happened. There wasn't much to say.

"We were just out walking the dog when we saw him. He was lying there on the sand. We asked him if he was okay. He said yes. He told us he was from Afghanistan. He said he came here on a boat. We called the police straightaway."

The truth as a lie. The policewoman had no reason to doubt him.

After taking down Dad's details and asking him if she could contact him if she had any further questions, we followed the police and Bashir back up to the road. An ambulance had arrived. Two paramedics took Bashir into their care and attended to him in the ambulance.

"Is he going to be okay?" Amy asked the policewoman.

"He'll be fine," she said.

The policewoman thanked us and said we could go, but we couldn't leave. We waited and watched as she went back to the ambulance and conferred with her colleague. Bashir, wrapped in a blanket, looked up to us and smiled sadly before turning away as if we were strangers. After that everything happened quickly. One of the paramedics jumped out of the ambulance and went to the front of the vehicle. The other closed the doors. The policeman stayed with Bashir while his female colleague went back to the patrol car, gave us a wave and got in. We watched as the two vehicles pulled away.

We drove home in silence. Amy sobbed quietly in the back seat. I thought about Bashir and all the things we had done together, about how he had become a part of our family. The worst thing was not being able to say goodbye.

The next day, before Dad left for Perth, he paid a visit to the detention centre in Coonawarra. I had to go to school, so

I couldn't join him, but he left a message on my phone before getting on the plane. He hadn't been able to see Bashir, as he'd predicted, but he did manage to speak to one of the security guys working there.

"I asked them to treat him well," Dad said in his message. "There's nothing more we can do."

Although Dad's attempt to become mayor of Darwin had failed, his name still carried weight in the community, and people respected him for the way he'd handled what the press had called "The Kiss & Tell Affair". The fact that Dad had gone to the detention centre and spoken to the people there could only be a good thing for Bashir. How many other refugees had a local politician taking interest in them?

It was strange coming home to an empty house that afternoon. The place felt like it was dead. No Dad. No Mum. No Bashir. Just Amy and me.

We ate the leftovers of the *Qabuli* and watched TV like a couple of zombies, not taking in what we were seeing. There was a ghost in the house that evening, the ghost of Bashir, and whatever we did, he seemed to be there with us. When Amy cuddled Toohey, it was Bashir's hand I saw stroking Toohey's head. When we zapped past a rugby game on TV, I knew that Bashir would have liked to have watched it. Even the food tasted of him.

I felt like I was waiting, but I didn't know what for. Waiting to hear from Bashir? Waiting for him to come back? I knew there was no reason to wait. Nothing was going to happen soon. It took months, even years, to process asylum seekers, especially when they had no papers. Unaccompanied minors like Bashir presented an additional problem. The government was worried that families from poor countries were sending their children to Australia so that they could follow on the grounds of family reunification rights. Instead of getting special treatment as an unaccompanied minor, UAMs (as they were called) were handled with even more caution than other asylum-seekers.

A couple of months ago I would have given anything to be at home on my own for a couple of days. Peace and quiet. Me doing exactly what I wanted, when I wanted, how I wanted. Eating what I wanted, watching what I wanted. Having friends around. Quality time. Now it just felt lonely.

Kate came around and tried to cheer me up, but she wasn't much help. She was as miserable as I was. Neither of us knew if we would ever see Bashir again.

A few days later, Mum and Dad came home. It was great to see them back. They seemed happy. I'd never really doubted they would sort things out. There was no way they were going to separate over a stupid kiss. It was just the humiliating way it came out that hurt the most.

They told us they'd talked things over, that they were good. What had happened wasn't a bad thing, they said. It was an opportunity. A tidal wave had come along and tried to sweep them apart, but they'd stuck together and now felt stronger for it. It was time to make some changes, to focus on what was important and be a family again. Less work, more play. Dad said he wanted to run for election again, but that next time he would do it differently. Mum said he would win.

I should have been happy. I was, really, but it was difficult to make sense of life with so many things going on. Bashir hovered over everything like a giant question mark. Did I have a right to be happy when Bashir was locked up somewhere down the road? What had I done to deserve a better life? Why was I lucky and Bashir not? Our family had managed to get through the crisis because we were together. Bashir was all on his own.

I asked Dad if we could go and see him. 5

"Listen, son," he said, his face twisted by a guilty conscience. "You have to remember he's just some kid we picked up on the beach. We don't know him. He's not our friend. We can't show too much interest in him, otherwise people will start asking questions." 10

"So what if they do?"

"There are millions of Bashirs out there. We can't help them all."

I managed to talk Dad around, and the next day we drove out to Coonawarra for one last time. The detention centre 15 was located just off the Stuart Highway, about a twenty-minute drive from our house. It had made headlines a couple of years back when ninety Afghan refugees escaped and held a peaceful protest on the Stuart Highway. I remembered seeing the pictures of the men with black beards sitting by the 20 roadside, proudly holding their hand-written banners, and the police looking all confused because the protestors made no effort either to escape or resist arrest. They just sat there by the road and waited for the TV cameras to come. Their message won a lot of sympathy, but it wasn't loud enough to 25 change anything.

The detention centre looked like an army barracks, surrounded by high fences. We pulled up at the front gate and pressed the intercom. A guard at the entrance came out to see us. He didn't recognise Dad. 30

"How can I help you, sir?" he asked.

Dad explained who we were and how we'd found one of the refugees washed up on the beach a week before. "We thought we'd pop around to pay him a visit. He seemed like a pleasant boy. Any chance of seeing him?"

5 The guard shook his head. "No."

"Can you give him a message from us?"

"No, sir, I can't."

The guard looked down into the car with a face like a rock. His eyelids were half closed.

10 "Do you know who I am?" Dad asked, removing his sunglasses.

"You said your name was Matthew Jackson."

"That's right," Dad said. "Candidate for Mayor. Alderman of the City of Darwin. I am just asking you to give one of the 15 refugees a message from us. Why is that a problem?"

"Because the client in question is not here."

Dad gave an uncomfortable laugh. "What?"

"Bashir Sadiqi. The kid from Afghanistan? Bloody good English? He left last night. He's been relocated to Nauru. 20 Took the night flight after signing the agreement."

"What agreement?"

"The one that says he was leaving Australia of his own free will."

I was about to say something but Dad raised his hand to 25 silence me.

"Thanks for the information. Have a nice day!" he said and rolled up the window before putting the car into reverse. A cloud of dust swirled up around us as we backed up to the road, the wheels of the car spinning.

30 "Bashir would never have left of his own free will!" I said, my heart pounding with outrage.

Dad gritted his teeth as he turned onto the highway and worked his way through the gears. "It's standard procedure. They wake you up in the middle of the night. They take you to a plane. They tell you to sign a piece of paper. It's loud. It's dark. You're scared. Anybody would sign it. You and I would 5 sign it. There's no other choice."

"So that's it?" I said. "Bashir's gone?"

Dad nodded grimly. "That's right. Bashir is gone."

2

I didn't sleep last night. I didn't eat all day. I stayed in my tent, not daring to leave, thinking about the Taliban man. 10

What should I do? Report him to the guards? They will not believe me. They always think we are lying. If we are sick, they think we are trying to trick them. If we ask for help, they are suspicious.

What can I do? Kill him before he kills me? 15

I cannot kill someone!

Ask someone in the camp to kill him for me?

As if that would be better!

Someone has to help me.

I decided to go and see Mister Thompson. Smiling Mister 20 *Thompson. Nice Mister Thompson. Kind Mister Thompson. My immigration case manager is in Australia on vacation. I cannot wait for her to come back. Mister Thompson is my only hope.*

I saw him sitting in the office at the entrance to RPC 1. I knocked on the door and asked if I could speak to him alone. 25 *We went around the back of the building.*

I told him about the man in RPC 2, the Taliban commander who had killed my father, about the bomb that had saved my life, about the danger I was in.

"This man is not a refugee," I told him. "He is a murderer."

5 Mister Thompson listened to my story and then shook his head. "No one here is a refugee until their status is confirmed," he said. "You are all asylum seekers. Some of you will be granted asylum. Others not. In the meantime, everyone here is equal."

"But this man, he did not leave his country because of dan-
10 ger," I insisted.

"So why is he here?"

"I do not know. Maybe he has relatives in Australia. Maybe he thinks he can get rich here. Maybe he is a terrorist."

Mister Thompson thought about this for a moment, then he
15 sighed. "We can't arrest him. We can't deport people without proof."

Proof? Where can I find proof?

There was only one answer.

"Can you take a photo of him and send it to my mother?"
20 I asked Mister Thompson. I was so excited about my plan, I could hardly speak. I don't know why I didn't think of it before.

"You're joking, right?"

"My mother will find proof. My mother is clever. She will find people who can confirm who he is."

25 My mother would even talk to the Taliban if necessary. RPC 1 has internet. The guards call home every day. They skype with their families. It is no problem to send her a photo.

"Just one photo," I insisted. "I can take the photo if you give me your phone."

30 Mister Thompson shook his head. "That's not going to happen. Just relax, Bashir. As long as you're in RPC 3, you're safe.

Just keep your head down and stay out of his way. Who knows, you could be out of this camp in a couple of weeks."

That was it? That was the sum of his help? 'Keep your head down'? 'Stay out of his way'? 'Wait until your application comes through'? 5

Did he not understand the situation I was in? Did he not understand the danger? I could be here for months, stuck in this prison with my father's executioner.

"Please, Mister Thompson!" I called as he turned away, but Mister Thompson did not hear me. He walked off, turned the 10 corner and went back into the office.

*

Kate and I were angry. We'd helped put Bashir into the system, and now the system had cheated us. It was as cruel as the things that had made him come here in the first place.

I have always been proud of being Australian. I *am* proud 15 of being Australian. Now, for the first time in my life, I was ashamed of what my country was doing. I felt helpless – helpless in the face of events, helpless at the mercy of others. It made me angry. I'd never felt helpless before.

When I look at Australia, I see an amazing country. I look 20 at the people here and I'm proud to be one of them. I can completely understand why anyone would want to live here. I'm happy that not everyone does. I can also understand that the politicians in Canberra are scared of that very same idea, but at some point you have to stop seeing people like Bashir 25 as statistics and start seeing them as human beings.

I wanted Bashir to be a part of the Australia I loved, and I was ready to fight for it. I started reading about the detention

centre on Nauru, a small island, only 21 square kilometres in size, with a population of ten thousand people. There were about a thousand asylum-seekers living there, all claiming asylum in Australia. The camp was run by an Australian
5 security company called Transmead. The flight there from Darwin took about five hours. The whole thing sounded like a logistical nightmare.

I found reports made for the Government describing conditions on Nauru. The government had a special name
10 for the people being kept there: they were called "transferees". The detention camp wasn't a camp but a "Regional Processing Centre". Everything was wrapped in a language that made it sound reasonable.

I read letters to the Australian government, written by
15 refugees in broken English, full of desperation. There were reports by human rights organisations into the effects of detainment on the mental health of asylum-seekers, especially on children. Journalists were banned from going there. Doctors who had worked there were not allowed to talk
20 about their experiences. There were allegations of sexual abuse. I couldn't believe something like this was happening in my own country.

That was the point. It wasn't. It was happening a long way away.

25 Kate and I came up with an idea. We didn't just want to stand around feeling helpless. We wanted to *do* something. The idea was simple: If we couldn't go to Nauru, we would bring Nauru to Darwin. We would make our very own detention centre on the roof of our high school.

30 The main building had three storeys and a flat roof. Our plan was to take over the top floor and lock ourselves in.

From the third floor you could get onto the roof. We wanted everyone to see our demonstration, so we decided that we would hang banners from the roof. We were guaranteed publicity. It was one thing if ninety Afghan men staged a protest outside their detention centre; it was something else if a group of Australian school kids did the same on the roof of their high school. Plus I was Matthew Jackson's son. That alone would make headlines.

We decided our idea could only be effective if there were more of us than just Kate and me. There was strength in numbers. Most of our friends knew about me and Dad finding Bashir on the beach, now we also made sure they knew about what had happened to Bashir after he was detained. Most of our friends responded with sympathy, some with outrage. Others weren't at all interested. Once we'd found out who we could trust, we told them about our plan. We were surprised how many agreed to join us.

Soon we were a group of ten, big enough to draw attention to ourselves, with the promise of more to come. We started meeting in secret, making plans and delegating jobs. We checked out the roof after school. It was beautiful up there. You could see right over Fannie Bay, the army barracks on the left, East Point to the right. It was the perfect place to stage a protest. There was a fire escape on the side of the building. Someone came up with the idea of chaining our bike locks to it to block it off. We wanted to turn the roof into a fortress.

"Ideally we would all stay together for the first three days," Kate told the group. "After that, there are no obligations. Anyone who wants to leave can. We're not going to force anyone to stay."

The project began to snowball. First we were ten, then we were twenty, and just a few days before the protest began, there were twenty-five of us. Some of the kids I didn't even know. They were from classes in the years below us. Two of them even came from another school.

Graham was one of the few people who I didn't talk to about our plan. I had been successfully avoiding him since the TV debate, but a few days before the protest, he came up to me in school and said, "I heard about what you're doing. Was Bashir the guy in your backyard?"

I wasn't surprised that he'd put two and two together, but I was surprised that he hadn't said anything before. Graham was the only person who had seen Bashir at our house. His knowledge was potentially dangerous.

"I don't know what you're talking about," I told him.

"The son of your dad's friend. The one from Melbourne."

"Oh, him. He was just visiting."

"Seems like a strange coincidence to me: an Afghan in the backyard; a week later an Afghan on the beach. I didn't know there were so many Afghans in Australia."

"There's lots of everything in Australia."

"Don't worry. I'm not going to tell anyone."

"No one would believe you if you did."

"You're right about that!" He smiled and changed the subject: "Are you still looking for people to help out?"

The question surprised me. "Why?"

"I wanted to ask if I could join you."

Join us? Graham Barton? Was this a trick?

"I'm really sorry about what happened with your dad," he said. "I shouldn't have told my dad about it."

I didn't say anything.

"My brother saw them together. We weren't going to say anything, but when you chucked me out of your house, I thought …"

"Just forget about it," I told him. It wasn't his fault.

"I'm tired of feeling guilty," he said, and it took me a moment to realise he wasn't talking about my dad. "I mean, it's not my fault I was born here, is it?"

"No," I agreed. "It's not your fault."

"But maybe it is in a way. I always used to think it's not my problem, but it is, isn't it? We're all part of this world. It belongs to all of us. So in a way it is my fault. I *am* responsible."

Responsible? That was a word I'd never expected to hear from Graham.

"You've been smoking too much weed."

"It was him in your backyard, right?" he said. "Bashir was staying with you?"

I couldn't tell if Graham just felt sorry about what he'd done to my family or if he genuinely wanted to help, but Kate said it didn't matter as long as he left his drugs at home. "The more, the merrier," was her motto.

"I'll talk to Kate," I promised him.

When I talked to her about Graham, she said he should come along. Now we were twenty-six.

It didn't take us long to get our gear together. We organised a couple of garden tents to provide shelter on the roof. We packed boxes with food and water. We had two stoves, plastic dishes, sleeping bags, mats. We even bought our own toilet paper. We had padlocks for the doors and banners for the roof. We started smuggling everything up to the third floor bit by bit, day after day, and stored it in a cupboard

in the art room. We put the tents in a cubicle in the boys' toilets and put up an OUT OF ORDER sign. We took the rest directly onto the roof on Friday afternoon when, instead of going home, we took up position on the third floor, all
5 twenty-six of us, and padlocked the doors from the inside.

The protest had begun.

3

There is only one way to protect myself: I have to get a photograph to Pakistan. There is no point in speaking to anyone here. If Mister Thompson doesn't believe me, no one will.

10 *We are not allowed cell phones in the camp, but once every two weeks, we go to RPC 1 to make a phone call. I call my mother. I tell her I am fine. She does her best to sound like she believes me, but I know she doesn't. It's like a game between us. I tell her I am well, and she tells me she is happy for me. I am*
15 *sure she is worried sick.*

When I lived in RPC 2, there was a man who had a phone. A Somali. Everyone knew about him. Everyone wanted to be friends with him. In the camp, we are not allowed to buy and sell things to each other. Nor are we allowed to exchange goods.
20 *We are given money which we can spend in the camp shop only. If we exchange goods, we are punished. Still it happens. Even the guards exchange things with us.*

I went to the canteen for dinner this evening. It was the first time I ate since yesterday morning. We are not allowed to take
25 *food out of the canteen, so all day yesterday I was hungry. All day today, my stomach ached, a hole getting bigger and bigger.*

In the canteen I did as Mister Thompson told me: I kept my head down. I looked out for the Taliban, but I didn't see him. I kept my eyes open for the Somali. He came into the canteen for the second shift.

I watched him while he ate. I waited until he finished his 5 *food. When he stood up, I stood up. When he left the tent, I followed him outside. Before he went back to RPC 2, I stopped him at the gate.*

"Do you have a phone?" I asked him. There were no guards around. 10

"Why you ask, boy?"

"I need to take a photo."

"Then buy a camera."

"I need to send it to someone."

He smiled. "A girl back home?" 15

"I cannot tell you why. Please, you must help me."

"What will you give me?"

"I can give you a spare T-shirt. I can do your washing for you."

"That is all?" 20

"I have nothing more to give."

He looked at me from head to toe and smiled. "Everybody has something to give."

I thought of the butterfly Saba gave me. I took it out of my pocket and showed it to him. 25

"Here! A gift that will lift your heart!"

The Somali just laughed. "You think like a child! Think like a man." He touched his trousers between his legs. "You know what you can give me. My phone is here when you want it."

*

We had a party that evening. There was no alcohol, no drugs, but we were all on a high. The adrenalin kicked in as we climbed onto the roof, and it didn't wear off for hours. We were on top of the world, watching the sundown over Fannie
5 Bay, music playing, talking and laughing, driven by the thrill of the fugitive, but with right on our side. There was nothing we could do wrong.

We tied our banners to the rooftop and swung them over the side of the building: FREE BASHIR, one of them said.
10 NO CHILDREN IN DETENTION. ASYLUM IS A HUMAN RIGHT. We put up a sign on the front of the building so that people could see it from the entrance: DARWIN DETEN-TION CENTRE. Kate and I had printed a mega-poster of Bashir which we unrolled and hung up on the antenna. It
15 was a photo I'd taken of him with one of his Lego master-pieces. Bashir was smiling proudly into the camera next to the wave-like roof of the Sydney Opera House.

It took the caretaker about an hour before he spotted us. By then all the banners and signs and posters were hang-
20 ing, our tents had been tied down, and our kitchen had been set up in the science lab. Mr Gilbert called up to us, but we couldn't understand him. A few minutes later he was bang-ing against the door at the top of the stairs. We went down to talk to him. We could see his silhouette on the other side
25 of the frosted glass, rattling the door handle, but the chain was padlocked.

"What do you think you're doing?" Gily shouted through the glass.

"Read the signs!" someone told him.

30 "You open this door right now or I'm going to call the principal!"

Of course, we were quite happy for Mr Gilbert to call the principal. We expected nothing less. We went back up to the roof and waited for Mrs Kim's car to appear. It pulled into the car park twenty minutes later. Gily ran up to her as Mrs Kim got out of the car looking confused. He followed her up to ⁵ the third floor.

"I admire your convictions," she told us from the other side of the glass, "but you won't achieve anything by this. I suggest you open the door and come down from the roof so that we can talk about this like civilized human beings." ¹⁰

Come down from the roof? Civilized human beings? After all the work we put in? Who did she think we were? Little kids who got cold feet when Mommy caught them being naughty? Besides, what was civilized about Nauru?

We said nothing, which only infuriated her more. There ¹⁵ was nothing to say. Our message was written on our banners.

"I have to remind you that you are trespassing on public property," Mrs Kim said, her anger rising. "The school is closed from Friday evening until Monday morning. You are ²⁰ breaking the law."

Twenty-six kids. Not a word. Someone in the group giggled.

"If you are going to behave like children then we will treat you like children!" Mrs Kim snapped. "I will expel you all!" ²⁵

Half an hour later, the police were on the scene. They looked up at the roof, perplexed. We saw them talking to Mrs Kim. Gily was running around the schoolyard like a headless chicken, bringing coffee to the cops. It didn't take long for the first news teams to turn up. ABD. TND. Local news net- ³⁰ works only. Parents and kids started flooding in to school to see what all the fuss was about. We were feeding Facebook and Twitter with constant updates. Most of the kids from our year group were there. I saw Mum and Dad in the crowd.

"Come down from the roof!" a policeman ordered through a megaphone, but we just waved back.

We watched the news on TV and the Internet. "Son of former candidate for mayor, Matthew Jackson, is one of the protestors," they claimed. "The campaign is said to be connected to the removal of teenage Afghan refugee, Bashir Sadiqi, from the Australian mainland after he was recently found on Casuarina Beach by Mr Jackson and his son. Sadiqi was sent to a regional processing centre on the island of Nauru just ten days ago."

The police sent someone up to the third floor to talk to us, a woman by the name of Jody. She sounded nice. She said she was a professional hostage negotiator.

"We don't have any hostages," Kate told her.

"I am aware of that," Jody replied in a calm voice. "It's my job to talk to people in pressure situations like this and find out what they want. So tell me, how can I help you?"

We'd written a kind of manifesto that we slipped under the door. Jody read it out loud: "*We demand the release of Bashir Sadiqi from the Nauru Regional Processing Centre and his return to the Australian mainland for processing. We call on the Australian government to relocate all families with children and UAMs in offshore detention centres back to the mainland.* That's it?" Jody asked after finishing. "That's all you want?"

We thought it was a reasonable request too. We weren't calling for the camps to be closed, though we thought they should be. We just wanted to get vulnerable people like Bashir out of there.

On the back of the page we'd outlined our suggestions in more detail: we believed there were plenty of families like mine and Kate's who would take in a family or a UAM while their application was being processed. The small numbers of children and families in question could easily be accom- 5 modated by the local population. We were talking about a couple of hundred people, not thousands. There was no need to send them away.

The truth was, even if our arguments were reasonable, they weren't going to result in change. We all knew that. 10 We weren't naïve. The offshore Regional Processing Centres existed as a deterrent to illegal immigrants. They were part of a larger picture that sent a clear message to people thinking about undertaking the dangerous journey: *If you try to come to our country illegally by boat, we will make sure you* 15 *never set foot here. Don't do it. Don't even think about it. You won't get what you want, so don't try.*

None of us believed the government was going to give in to a bunch of teenagers from the Northern Territory, but we figured we could make some waves. 20

"I'll see what I can do," said Jody through the glass door.

Jody soon appeared on TV, providing reporters with information. She described us as "courageous young people with a strong sense of justice". She promised to communi- cate our demands to the Department of Immigration and 25 Border Protection in Melbourne. It almost felt like she was on our side.

As the evening went on and the crowd began to disperse, the thrill of the afternoon's events started to wear off. Night fell, and it occurred to me that some things were the same 30 wherever you are. Night is always night, whether in Nauru,

Australia or Pakistan. Sleep is sleep. It was a comforting thought.

When the others went downstairs to sleep in the classrooms, Kate and I took the first shift on the roof. We didn't think the police would try to remove us by force, but we decided to post a watch just in case. If the cops did try to come in, we'd agreed not to resist arrest. As many of us as possible would try to lock ourselves into the science lab and continue our protest there. We didn't want to make it too easy for them.

As Kate and I lay there on the roof that night, gazing up at the night sky, the sound of the city humming in the distance, Kate said, "I wonder what Bashir is doing right now."

4

When I woke up this morning, I felt something at the foot of my bed. I looked under the sheet and found a small plastic bag. Inside was a cell phone. I could hardly believe my eyes. A note was lying next to it. It was from Mister Thompson. "Take the photo and leave the phone under the trash cans by 4 pm," it said. "Write your mother a note and take a photo of it. Enter her number under "mum". Code for the phone is 7414. Burn this note."

Now that I had the phone in my hand, I was gripped by panic. My heart started beating so hard, it almost hurt. My legs went weak. Can I do this? How can I take a photograph of my father's murderer without him seeing me? It seemed an impossible task. Why hadn't I thought about this before?

I burned the note and thought things through. I had to be careful. If a guard saw me, I could get into trouble. The best place to get a photo of the Taliban was inside the canteen, but I would have to get close enough to him to see his face. He would see me for sure. He might recognise me. That was the risk I 5 *was going to have to take. If I was lucky, he wouldn't. The most important thing was that I get his picture without him seeing the camera.*

All morning I practised taking photos as inconspicuously as possible, slipping the phone out of my pocket and holding it 10 *close to my hip, pressing the button with my thumb, rehearsing, improving, finding the best angle. After a while, I had the routine down to perfection. I could carry the phone in my pocket, unlock it with my fingers, remove it, and take a photo without looking down once.* 15

I was ready.

I went to the canteen ten minutes before the first lunch shift. A guard saw me and laughed. "Waiting will only make you hungrier!" he said. He did not realise that I was not there for the food but because I wanted to be the first inside. I didn't want to 20 *miss the Taliban. I only had one chance.*

When the first lunch shift started, I took my tray and sat down in the corner of the canteen. I could see the entrance from there. I hoped I wouldn't have to wait until the second lunch shift. I was so nervous, I could hardly eat. 25

I didn't have to wait long. The Taliban came into the canteen after ten minutes. I bowed my head so that he didn't see me. The canteen was half full. I watched him out of the corner of my eye as he queued up for his food and took his tray to a table. He sat down with his back to me. 30

I finished my food and took my tray back. I had to approach the Taliban from the front, so I circled the tent and walked slowly towards him from the other side. He was eating hungrily, his head bowed over his plate. If he didn't look up, I wouldn't get
5 *the photo I needed.*

I had to do something.

Just before I passed by his table, I dropped Saba's butterfly onto the floor. The Taliban looked up, surprised by the sound. I bent down to pick up the butterfly, slipped the phone out of my
10 *pocket and took the photo as I stood back up. At the same time I held out the butterfly to show the Taliban. He looked at it, then to me, and I saw his eyes narrow for the fraction of a second before he turned back to his food to continue eating. The whole thing lasted no more than a few seconds.*

15 *As I left the canteen, I didn't dare look back.*

When I got back to my tent, I checked the photo. It was perfect. The Taliban's face was clear, the scar on his forehead, food on his lips. I entered my mother's number, put the phone into the plastic bag, and took it to the trash cans.

*

20 The next day, we were all over the news. Nationwide. Worldwide. ABC. SBS. BBC. CNN. We were even on Al Jazeera. People were blogging about us, posting pictures of our school, discussing our manifesto. The press was talking about a "Young Australian Revolution" and called us "The Kids on
25 the Block". The term "UAM" became an instant hashtag. Tweets were crossing oceans and breaking down borders to discuss what was now a worldwide problem. Many agreed that sovereign nations were a great thing, but how could

borders work in the long term? Where was the humanity in them?

A Facebook group called "Australia Says NO to Immigrants" described us as "irresponsible teenagers with no idea about the realities of modern-day politics". They said we were "naive idealists" who only saw one side of the story. They listed the problems illegal immigrants brought with them. They pointed out that Australia had a right to protect its own borders and that the number of deaths at sea had dropped as a result of policy. Their arguments were easy to understand, but there was so much hatred behind their words.

In the afternoon, Graham came up to me and told me that my dad was asking for me. I went down to the third floor and saw his shadow on the other side of the glass.

"Hi Dad."

"Hi Cooper. How are things?"

"Good."

"Pretty impressive operation you've got going here."

"Thanks."

"How long are you going to keep this up for?"

"I don't know. A while."

I saw Dad's silhouette nodding. He stepped closer to the door, his cheek almost touching the glass. He lowered his voice. "Is there anything I can do?"

I don't know if I was surprised by his conspiratorial tone or the frankness of his question, but I didn't know what to say.

"Do you need anything?" he asked, his voice hushed.

"No. We're fine. Just … don't be angry with me, okay?"

"Angry?" he said. "I'm not angry with you. I'm proud of you, son! I think it's amazing what you're doing. I wish there was something I could do."

His face pulled away from the door as a woman's high heels came clicking up the tiles of the stairwell. I heard Jody's voice.

"Mr Jackson. Nice to see you."

A few hours later, it was Dad who was making waves on the Australian networks. ABC announced BREAKING NEWS. *Ex-candidate Matthew Jackson admits to having harboured an illegal immigrant in his home while campaigning to become mayor of Darwin.* Dad gave an exclusive interview to ABC in which he told the whole story, about how I'd found Bashir that night on the beach and hidden him until Dad discovered us, about how Bashir had lived with us and why we'd staged his arrival for a second time.

"We miss him," Dad said. "That's what this is all about."

Dad said he knew he was making himself liable by going public, that the police would no doubt press charges, but he told his interviewer it was time to tell the full story. He quoted our school motto *esse quam videri* ("to be, rather than to seem to be") and said it was time to do just that: to tell things as they were.

Suddenly, the issue had become an emotional one. Why was Bashir being locked up when there was a family in Darwin who was happy to take him? How many other people were suffering unnecessarily in this way? Australians began to speak up and offer their help. The practicality of the Pacific Solution was put into question. Was it really effective? How much were the offshore detention centres costing? Was Australia avoiding its international responsibilities?

Dad became our man on the ground, the qualified voice of our campaign, and he knew how to talk politics.

We stayed on the roof that weekend watching Dad's meteoric rise in the Australian media, but down below the crowds began to lose interest. When Monday morning came, we were expecting school to be cancelled, but at half past seven the teachers arrived, followed shortly afterwards by the flow of kids. Business as usual was Mrs Kim's approach. She chose to ignore us. Jody turned up again on Monday afternoon, but she had little to say other than, "I've sent your request to the DIBP. I'll let you know what they say." Even Mr Gilbert stopped looking up to the roof to see us. By Tuesday the first camera teams began to leave. The party mood was over. On Wednesday the first people left the protest. They'd stuck it out for five days. There was no shame in leaving. The next day more followed. By Friday afternoon, after a week of protest, there were only six of us left. On Saturday only three remained: Kate, Graham and I.

That night Kate posed the question we were all thinking about: "How much longer do you think we should stay here?"

Graham shrugged his shoulders. "Until they release Bashir?"

"That's not going to happen," I told him. "We've made our point. Things are not going to get any better. We should leave in the morning."

And that is what we did. Enough was enough.

5

I didn't see Mister Thompson for the next couple of days. I stayed in RPC 3, moving around the compound like a ghost, only leaving for breakfast. The first breakfast shift of the day was usually attended by families. I felt safer then. Most of the single men
5 *stayed in bed and took the second breakfast shift when things were quieter. I didn't want to risk seeing the Taliban man. I ate no lunch or dinner for days.*

Eventually I couldn't stand it any longer. It wasn't just the smell of cooked food wafting through the camp in the evenings,
10 *it was the fact I didn't know if Mister Thompson had kept his promise. I needed to know if he had done what he had said.*

I went to RPC 1, but Mister Thompson wasn't in the office. I checked out the canteen, walked up to the front gates, circled back over the dusty yard. No sign of him anywhere.

15 *A big guard called Mr Nicolls was sitting outside the office, drinking water. I went up to him and asked him if I could speak to Mister Thompson.*

"No, you can't," he said. "He's not here."

"Where is he?"

20 *"Back home."*

Home? "When is he coming back?"

Nicolls laughed. "If he's got any common sense, he won't be coming back at all. He's been transferred to the mainland."

My breath left me. I felt like I was suffocating. Mister Thomp-
25 *son had left? What would happen to me?*

"I have to speak to him," I told Nicolls. "It's urgent."

Nicolls stood up, stretching himself tall in front of me. "Everything's urgent around here," he said and pulled up his trousers. He threw his empty water bottle into a bin.

"Please, Mr Nicolls. It really is very important."

"You're starting to get on my nerves, Bashir. Go back to your tent and get some sleep. You look like hell."

"There's a murderer in this camp!" I said, but it didn't sound real coming out of my mouth. 5

"I bet there are lots of murderers in this camp. That's why you're here: so we can find out which of you are scum. Now go on! Get back to RPC3!"

I turned away. My head was burning from the midday sun.

"And if I don't see you before the weekend, happy birthday!" 10 *Nicolls added as I walked away.*

Happy birthday? What was he talking about?

Only then did I remember. Nicolls was right. It's my birthday next week. I'm turning eighteen. Although I lost my passport, I never lied about my date of birth. After they accepted my status 15 *as a minor, they must have entered my date of birth officially.*

But soon I will no longer be a minor, and as a single male, they will send me back to Bravo camp.

Eighteen years old. I hope it is not my last birthday.

*

When we came down from the roof that Sunday morn- 20 ing there was a reception committee waiting for us. We'd announced our decision by Twitter, and a small crowd had gathered in the car park. As we unlocked the doors, Jody took us under her wing. "Hi, guys," she said with a smile. "You did well." She swept us downstairs and shielded us from the 25 camera teams. Journalists bombarded us with questions which we didn't answer because everything was so unbearably loud. We just wanted to go home, to our families, to our beds, to a long, hot shower. It had been fun at the beginning, but being locked up is not healthy for anyone, even if you choose to do it yourself.

Our principal decided to make a show of her generosity. The following day Mrs Kim announced she was going to forgive those protestors who had left the campaign of their own free will, but in Kate, Graham and myself she saw the ringleaders who needed to be punished. She said she would not press charges, but she felt obliged to expel all three of us.

"Cooper rejected my authority," she wrote in a letter to my parents. "Without respect for my position as principal, I can see no place for him here in Darwin High School. I wish him all the best with his academic future."

We had rocked the boat. Now we were having to pay the price for it.

I felt empty in the days after the protest came to end. My head ached. I had no appetite. We hadn't achieved anything. Bashir was still on Nauru. Kate was grounded. Her parents refused to let her see me. Graham disappeared. He didn't answer his phone. He wasn't even online. When I went around to his house, nobody came to the door. After having spent a week with friends twenty-four hours a day, I was now on my own.

At home Mum kept bursting into tears. Dad was facing criminal charges. I'd flunked school in my last year. Mum blamed us for having taken things too far. "Bashir should never have moved in with us," she kept saying. "I knew it was a mistake from the very beginning. Now look at us! It's a bloody mess!"

Dad told her not to worry. His lawyer said he would probably get away with a fine and some community service. His public image remained unharmed. A lot of people admired him for what he had done.

As for me, being expelled wasn't the end of the word, and the police let me off with a warning. There were other colleges in Darwin. If they didn't take me, the private schools would. 5

Eventually the media hype died down. People lost interest in Dad. The public debate about offshore detention centres took a back seat after a Muslim rebel group kidnapped hundreds of schoolgirls in Nigeria. Obama and Putin were at 10 loggerheads over the Crimea. Back home, the reality of daily life kicked in. Kate's parents enrolled her in a girl's boarding school in Brisbane. She planned to move there after the semester break.

I had a couple of interviews at local colleges. They all 15 rejected me. Mum dragged me to some private schools to meet the principals, but I could tell they didn't like me either. In the end we decided it would be better to make a clean start and for me to go and stay with Auntie Claire in Melbourne. She was happy to take me in, and there were plenty 20 of schools in Melbourne that didn't care who I was.

It was a big comedown after the protest, a major crashlanding, but I knew it would pass. Life goes on – even without Kate, even without school, even if we did fail to get Bashir out of the camp. 25

One morning, a week or so later, I woke up late and realised it was Bashir's birthday. It was Anzac Day, so it was an easy date to remember. There were lots of reports on the radio about Australian military actions around the word, past and present, and the fallen soldiers which Anzac Day 30 honoured. Bashir was turning eighteen, but I wouldn't be able to congratulate him.

I was at home on my own, making myself breakfast, when the phone rang. Our house phone never rang during the day. If my parents wanted to reach me, they called me on my mobile. Everyone knew they were out. There was no reason to call the house.

I looked at the display. I didn't recognise the number. It looked foreign to me.

I answered. "Hello?"

"Hi, Cooper!"

The line crackled. The voice died.

"Hello? Who's there?"

"Cooper? Can you hear me?"

The caller sounded a million miles away, but I recognised his voice immediately. "Bashir?"

"Hi, Cooper, how are you?"

I hadn't spoken to Bashir for more than two months, but he only had to say a few words and it was as if he'd never gone away. I could see his smiling face before me.

"I'm good. And you? Where are you?"

"I'm calling from Nauru. I need your help."

"Okay. What can I do?"

"I need you to find a man for me. His name is Stuart Thompson. He works for a company called Transmead."

I grabbed a pen and started writing. "Stuart with a 'u' or a 'w'?"

"With a 'u'. And Thompson with a 'p'. Transmead Services."

I remembered the name from my research. Transmead was the company that ran the camp on Nauru.

"What's this about?"

There was another crackle on the line.

"I cannot tell you on the phone." I could hear the fear in Bashir's voice. "You have to find him. Soon."

"Do you know where he lives?" 5

"I think in Brisbane, but he could be anywhere now."

"What do you want me to I tell him?"

"He has something I need. He will know what."

"Okay. I'll get onto it."

"Thanks, Cooper. I have to go. My time is up." 10

"How can I contact you?"

"If Mister Thompson has what I need, you will find a way. Goodbye, Cooper. And thank you again."

"Wait!" I called before Bashir hung up. "Happy birthday!"

But the line was already dead. 15

6

I took a long time to pack my things this morning. I took my T-shirts and folded them again and again. I packed them and unpacked them ten times.

I cleaned Saba's butterfly until the wings gleamed in the sun-light. I was waiting for the guards to come and get me. Today 20 *was the day I had to move back into RPC 2. For the last two days now I have been an adult in the eyes of the law.*

The guards came to get me after lunch. They didn't say much. "Let's go," that is all. I followed them. They showed me my new bed in Bravo. It looked the same as my old one. I spent 25 *all afternoon lying on it, staring up at the ceiling, watching the flies. I didn't want to move. I wanted to be invisible.*

I had just closed my eyes and was drifting off to sleep when someone spoke to me in Pashto. "May I sit down?"

I opened my eyes. The Taliban was standing next to me, looking down at my bed. My heart stopped beating.

5 "You are Afghan?" he asked.

I nodded. I couldn't speak.

"A fellow countryman!" he said proudly and sat down without waiting for an invitation. "How long have you been here?"

I propped myself up on my elbows. I wanted to jump up and 10 run away, but there was nowhere to run to.

"Two months."

"That is a long time, my friend," he said, shaking his head as a sign of his sympathy. "It was a mistake to come to Australia. This new law is very bad. If I had known about it, I would have 15 never have tried to come here. I could have gone to Germany. Were you on a boat?"

"Yes."

"Christmas Island?"

"No. Darwin."

20 "Darwin?" he repeated the name as if trying to find it on a map in his mind. "Darwin? Darwin? Like the scientist?"

"Yes, sir. A city in northern Australia."

"I see. Where is your family?"

"They live in Pakistan."

25 He raised an eyebrow. "In Quetta?"

"Yes, sir."

"Oh. A dangerous city."

I sat up and swung my feet to the ground. "Please excuse me, sir. I have to go to the toilet."

30 I stood up, but the man grabbed my wrist.

"Wait. I am not finished yet. We have to talk."

He didn't let go of my arm. I sat back down.

He put his arm around my shoulder and whispered into my ear: "I know who you are."

I tried to stand up again, but the man held me down. His grip tightened around my wrist, his other hand on my shoulder. 5

"I have enough blood on my hands," he said. "I do not want more. We must let go of the past, my friend, otherwise we have a problem."

He pressed his fingernails into my arm and my shoulder as if he wanted to draw blood. 10

"Can you let go of the past?" he asked me, his lips still close to my ear.

I nodded. "Yes."

"That is good. For every problem there is a solution. I am happy we have an understanding." He let go of my arm. "Then 15 *we are agreed."*

I stood up. "You must excuse me," I said. "I have to go."

He looked at me with his deep black eyes, searching my face as if trying to decide whether he could trust me, but it was too late. I had already betrayed him. I looked away. I didn't want 20 *him to see the betrayal in my eyes. I hurried out of the tent before he changed his mind.*

✤

I once read somewhere that there are around a hundred billion birds on the planet. I'll just say that figure again: one 25 hundred billion. Now I know that birds are a lot smaller than human beings, and they don't eat as much meat as we do, but it still makes for an interesting comparison: a hundred billion birds compared to seven billion people.

Those hundred billion birds all have their places of habitat, their resting places and their homes, their breeding
5 grounds and feeding places, the places they migrate to in winter, the places they stay in the summer, but one thing they don't have is borders. This planet belongs to all of them, whether they're sparrows or eagles, parrots or flamingos. Maybe that's why birds don't fight. Maybe that's why birds
10 don't kill each other. Birds are, well, just birds. They might not be as clever as human beings, but they'll probably outlive us.

After Bashir's call, I went straight to my dad's office. It took him less than an hour to track down Stuart Thompson. A few
15 phone calls to the right people, and he soon had his address, driver's licence number and cell phone. I was impressed.

Thompson was working at a detention centre in Adelaide. Dad called him there and put the phone on loudspeaker. He knew who my dad was as soon as he said his name.

20 "I read about you and your son in the newspaper," Thompson's voice sounded tired. "Our bosses ordered a news blackout during your campaign, but we all knew what you were doing. They said they didn't want any of the refugees to hear about it."

25 Thompson told us he had been transferred back to the mainland because one of his colleagues had reported him for improper conduct. He had lent his cell phone to one of the refugees and was facing disciplinary action. That person was Bashir. Thompson also told us the story behind why he'd
30 done it.

Bashir's mother had contacted Thompson a few days before our call. She'd sent him photos. They showed a bearded man with a Kalashnikov in his hand surrounded by Taliban fighters. Another showed him training men in black balaclavas. There was a photo of a document with the man's name on it: Akhtar Osmani, a former Taliban officer who had fallen out of favour with his commanders. Thompson said there was little doubt it was the same man, but he had no way to contact Bashir. Besides, he was scared. He risked losing his job. The fear had paralysed him.

But now there was a way.

"Send me the photos," Dad told him. "I'll deal with it from here."

Within minutes Dad had the photos on his cell phone and was making calls to the Department of Immigration and Border Protection. Half an hour later the Minister called him personally. It was just as Dad had expected: the situation was a PR dream. For the Minister, it confirmed the need to process all asylum-seekers carefully.

"We don't want criminals coming into Australia," he later told the press. "It is imperative that we find out who these people are before we let them into our country. Bashir Sadiqi and his family have done Australia a great service. We don't want the Taliban here."

The head of Transmead was quickly informed. Akhtar Osmani was removed from the camp and deported to Afghanistan. The Minister for Immigration fast-tracked Bashir's refugee status application and granted him a visa with the additional right of returning to mainland Australia. He was using Bashir for publicity, everybody knew it, but we didn't care. Bashir was free.

A few days later, Bashir landed at the airport to a storm of reporters, TV cameras and government officials. His case manager handed him over into our care. She later told us what Bashir had said when she'd told him the good news.

5   "You've been granted a full visa," were her words. "Is there anywhere in particular you would like to go?"

Apparently he didn't hesitate for a moment. "Darwin."

Bibliography & References

"Taking responsibility: conditions and circumstances at Australia's Regional Processing Centre in Nauru", Parliament of Australia, 31.10.2015

"The Forgotten Children: National Inquiry into Children in Immigration Detention", Australian Human Rights Commission (AHRC), November 2014: The report includes more than 50 submissions from minors in the detention centres on Nauru and Manus Islands.

"Leaving Family Behind: understanding the irregular migration of UAMs", Australian Government, Department of Immigration and Border Protection (DIBP), December 2014

"This is breaking people: human rights violations at Australia's asylum seeker processing centre on Manus Island, Papua New Guinea", Amnesty International, December 2013

Fact sheets, website of The Refugee Council of Australia

Fact sheets, website of The Department of Immigration and Border Protection

Website of Roads to Refuge

Website of ChilOut (children out of immigration detention)

Vocabulary

Abbreviations
adj = adjective; jdm., jdn. = jemandem, jemanden; n = noun;
sb. = somebody; sth. = something; v = verb

A
abroad [ə'brɔːd] ins Ausland
abuse [ə'bjuːs] Missbrauch
(to) accommodate [ə'kɒmədeɪt]
    unterbringen
accusation [ˌækjuˈzeɪʃn] Anschul-
    digung
(to) accuse [ə'kjuːz] beschuldigen,
    vorwerfen
(to) ache [eɪk] wehtun
(to) achieve [ə'tʃiːv] erreichen
(to) adapt [ə'dæpt] sich anpassen
additional [ə'dɪʃənl] weitere
(to) adjust [ə'dʒʌst] sich anpassen
(to) admit [əd'mɪt] zugeben
(to) adore [ə'dɔː] anhimmeln
advanced [əd'vɑːnst] fortge-
    schritten
affair [ə'feə] Affäre
aftertaste ['ɑːftəteɪst] Nach-
    geschmack
afterwards ['ɑːftəwədz] danach
agreement [ə'griːmənt] Vertrag
air-conditioning ['eə kəndɪʃənɪŋ]
    Klimaanlage

alderman election [ɔːldəmən
    ɪ'lekʃn] Wahl des Stadtrats
alive [ə'laɪv] am Leben
allegation [ˌælə'geɪʃn] Behauptung
allegiance [ə'liːdʒəns] Zugehörig-
    keit
(to) allow [ə'laʊ] erlauben
almighty [ɔːl'maɪti] allmächtig
amazement [ə'meɪzmənt] Staunen
angel ['eɪndʒl] Engel
angle ['æŋgl] Blickwinkel
(to) announce [ə'naʊns] ankün-
    digen
anticipation [ænˌtɪsɪ'peɪʃn] Erwar-
    tung
anyway ['eniweɪ] sowieso
Anzac ['ænzæk] australisches und
    neuseeländisches Armeekorps
apparently [ə'pærəntli]
    anscheinend
(to) appear [ə'pɪə] erscheinen
application [kleɪm] Antrag
approach [ə'prəʊtʃ] Heransgehens-
    weise
armchair ['ɑːmtʃeə] Sessel
armed [ɑːmd] bewaffnet

army barracks [ɑːmi ˈbærəks] Kaserne

(to) arouse [əˈraʊz] wecken

arrangement [əˈreɪndʒmənt] Vereinbarung

ashamed [əˈʃeɪmd]: be ashamed sich schämen

astonishment [əˈstɒnɪʃmənt] Erstaunen

asylum seeker [əˈsaɪləm ˌsiːkə] Asylbewerber/in

attempt [əˈtempt] Versuch

(to) attend [əˈtend] besuchen; betreuen

attention [əˈtenʃn] Aufmerksamkeit

authorities [ɔːˈθɒrətiːz] Behörde

(to) avoid [əˈvɔɪd] vermeiden

awake [əˈweɪk] wach

aware [əˈweə] bewusst

awkward [ˈɔːkwəd] heikel

B

(to) back off [ˈbæk ɒf] sich zurückziehen

(to) back up [ˈbæk ʌp] rückwärts fahren

baffled [ˈbæfəld] ratlos

balance [ˈbæləns] Gleichgewicht

(to) bang [bæŋ] schlagen

(to) banish [ˈbænɪʃ] verbannen

bare [beə] nackt

barely [ˈbeəli] kaum

basement [ˈbeɪsmənt] Untergeschoss

bay window [beɪ ˈwɪndəʊ] Erkerfenster

beard [bɪəd] Bart

bearded [ˈbɪdɪd] bärtig

beforehand [bɪˈfɔːhænd] vorher

behaviour [bɪˈheɪvjə] Benehmen

(to) belong [bɪˈlɒŋ] hingehören; (to) belong to gehören

bend down [ˈbend daʊn] sich niederbeugen (bend, bent, bent)

besides [bɪˈsaɪdz] außerdem

(to) bet [bet] wetten

(to) betray [bɪˈtreɪ] verraten

betrayal [bɪˈtreɪəl] Verrat

billion [ˈbɪljən] Milliarde

birth [bɜːθ]: Geburt; give birth gebären

blackout [ˈblækaʊt] news blackout Nachrichtensperre

blank [blæŋk] ausdruckslos

blanket [ˈblæŋkɪt] Decke

blaze [bleɪz] Flamme, Glut

(to) blind [blaɪnd] blenden

block [blɒk] Kiez

(to) block off [blɒk ˈɒf] absperren

bloody [ˈblʌdi] verdammt

(to) blow [bləʊ] blasen (blow, blew, blown)

blunt [blʌnt] unverblümt

(to) boost [buːst] födern

border [ˈbɔːdə] Grenze

boss [bɒs] Vorgesetzte(r)

(to) bow [baʊ] beugen

(to) break [breɪk]: Give me a break! Verschon mich!

(to) break the law [breɪk ðə ˈlɔː] gegen das Gesetz verstoßen

breath [breθ] Atem(zug)

(to) breathe [briːð] atmen

breeding grounds [ˈbriːdɪŋ graʊndz] Brutstätte

(to) breeze [briːz] Brise

bright [braɪt] hell, leuchtend

broad [brɔːd] breit

broadcast [ˈbrɔːdkɑːst] übertragen

(to) bug [bʌg] auf die Nerven gehen

bullshit [ˈbʊlʃɪt] Mist, Quatsch

bunch [bʌntʃ] Bündel; Haufen; Gruppe

burden [ˈbɜːdn] Last

(to) burst [bɜːst] ausbrechen

(to) bury [ˈberi] begraben

button [ˈbʌtn] Knopf

C

caller [ˈkɔːlə] Anrufer/in

(to) calm down [kɑːm daʊn] sich beruhigen

calmness [ˈkɑːmnəs] Gelassenheit

(to) campaign [kæmˈpeɪn] einen Wahlkampf führen

(to) cancel [ˈkænsl] absagen

canoe (n) [kəˈnuː] Kanu; (v) Kanu fahren

capable [ˈkeɪpəbl] fähig

carbon tax [ˈkɑːbən tæks] Kohlenstoffsteuer

(to) care [keə]: (to) care about sb. sich um jdn. kümmern

caretaker [ˈkeəteɪkə] Hausmeister/in

carpet [ˈkɑːpɪt] Teppich

(to) carry [ˈkæri] tragen

(to) carry weight [kæri ˈweɪt] Einfluss haben

carton [ˈkɑːtn]: carton of milk Milchtüte

case [keɪs] just in case für alle Fälle

case manager [ˈkeɪs mænɪdʒə] Sachbearbeiter/in

(to) cast [kɑːst] werfen

casual [ˈkæʒuəl] gleichgültig

catch [kætʃ] Haken

(to) cause [kɔːz] verursachen

caution [ˈkɔːʃn] Vorsicht; Warnung

cautiously [ˈkɔːʃəsli] vorsichtig

ceiling [ˈsiːlɪŋ] Decke

(to) chain [tʃeɪn] anketten

(to) chant [tʃɑːnt] rufen

charges [ˈtʃɑːdʒəz]: press charges Anklage erheben

cheat [tʃiːt] (n) Betrüger/in; (v) betrügen

cheekbones [ˈtʃiːkbəʊnz] Wangenknochen

chess [tʃes] Schach

chest [tʃest] Brust

(to) chuck out [tʃʌk ˈaʊt] herausschmeißen

chunk [tʃʌŋk] Stück

(to) circle [ˈsɜːkl] kreisen

(to) claim [kleɪm] beantragen; behaupten

client [ˈklaɪənt] Kunde/Kundin

clock [klɒk] Uhr

coast guard [ˈkəʊst gɑːd] Küstenwach

cockroach [ˈkɒkrəʊtʃ] Kakerlake

coincidence [kəʊˈɪnsɪdəns] Zufall

(to) collapse [kəˈlæps] zusammenbrechen

colleague [ˈkɒliːg] Mitarbeiter/in

comedown [ˈkʌmdaʊn] Absturz

comforting [ˈkʌmfətɪŋ] beruhigend

commander [kəˈmɑːndə] Kommandant

(to) comment [ˈkɒment] sich aüßern

common sense [kɒmən ˈsens] gesunder Menschenverstand

complete [kəmˈpliːt] völlig

completely [kəmˈpliːtli] ganz, vollständig

condition [kənˈdɪʃn] Bedingung

conduct [kənˈdʌkt] Verhalten

(to) confer [kənˈfɜː] sich besprechen

confines [ˈkɒnfaɪnz] Grenzen

confirmation [ˌkɒnfəˈmeɪʃn] Bestätigung

confused [kənˈfjuːzd] verwirrt

(to) congratulate [kənˈgrætʃuleɪt] beglückwünschen

conscience [ˈkɒnʃəns] Gewissen

conspiratorial [kənˌspɪrəˈtɔːriəl] verschwörerisch

constant [ˈkɒnstənt] kontinuierlich

(to) construct [kənˈstrʌkt] bauen

(to) contain [kənˈteɪn] zügeln, bremsen

contents [ˈkɒntentz] Inhalte

controversial [ˌkɒntrəˈvɜːʃl] umstrittend

convention centre [kənˈvenʃn sentə] Kongresszentrum

conversation-killer [kɒnvəˈseɪʃn kɪlə] Killerfrage

conviction [kənˈvɪkʃn] Überzeugung

convinced [kənˈvɪnst] überzeugt

convincing [kənˈvɪnsɪŋ] überzeugend

coolness [ˈkuːlnəs] Kühle

cop [kɒp] Bulle, Polizist/in

core [kɔː] Kern

council [ˈkaʊnsl] Rat, Verband

(to) count [ˈkaʊnt]: (to) count on sth. sich auf etwas verlassen

counterpart [ˈkaʊntəpɑːt] Gegenstück

courageous [kəˈreɪdʒəs] mutig

covered [ˈkʌvəd] bedeckt

CPR [ˌsiː piː ˈɑː] Herz-Lungen-Wiederbelebung

(to) crackle [ˈkrækl] knistern

crash-landing [ˈkræʃ lændɪŋ] Bruchlandung

crate [kreɪt] Kiste

criminal [krɪmɪnl] (adj) strafrechtlich, kriminell; (n) Verbrecher/in; criminal record [krɪmɪnl ˈrekɔːd] Eintrag im Strafregister

(to) crisscross [ˈkrɪs krɒs] durchkreuzen

croc [krɒk] = crocodile

crowd [kraʊd] Menge

cruel [ˈkruːəl] unmenschlich

crumb [krʌm] Krümel

cubicle [ˈkjuːbɪkl] Kabine; Toilette

(to) cuddle [ˈkʌdl] kuscheln

curiosity [ˌkjʊəriˈɒsəti] Neugier

curious [ˈkjʊəriəs] neugierig

current affairs [kʌrənt əˈfeərz] aktuelle Ereignisse

D

daily [ˈdeɪli] täglich

(to) dare [deə] wagen

(to) darken [ˈdɑːkən] dunkel
werden

death [deθ] Tod, Todesfall

decision [dɪˈsɪʒn] Entscheidung

delighted [dɪˈlaɪtɪd] begeistert

demand [dɪˈmɑːnd] Foderung

demanding [dɪˈmɑːndɪŋ] schwierig

(to) demolish [dɪˈmɒlɪʃ] abreißen

dentist [ˈdentɪst] Zahnartz/ärtzin

(to) deny [dɪˈnaɪ] bestreiten

(to) deport [dɪˈpɔːt] abschieben

deranged [dɪˈreɪndʒd] gestört

deserted [dɪˈzɜːtɪd] menschenleer

(to) deserve [dɪˈzɜːv] verdienen

desire [dɪˈzaɪə] Lust

desperate [ˈdespərət] verzweifelt

desperation [ˌdespəˈreɪʃn]
Verzweiflung

(to) detain [dɪˈteɪn] festhalten

detainment [dɪˈteɪnmənt] Inhaf-
tierung

detention centre [dɪˈtenʃn ˈsentə]
Inhaftierungslager

deterrent [dɪˈterənt] Abschreckung

difficulty [ˈdɪfɪkəlti] Schwierigkeit

(to) dig [dɪg] stecken

dirt [dɜːt] Schmutz

(to) disappear [ˌdɪsəˈpɪə] ver-
schwinden

disapproval [ˌdɪsəˈpruːvl] Miss-
billigung

(to) disarm [dɪsˈɑːm] entwaffnen

disciplinary [ˈdɪsəplɪnəri] diszipli-
narisch

discomfort [dɪsˈkʌmfət] Unwohl-
sein

disgust [dɪsˈgʌst] Empörung

(to) disinfect [ˌdɪsɪnˈfekt] desinfi-
zieren

(to) disperse [dɪˈspɜːs] sich
auflösen

distance [ˈdɪstəns]: Ferne; keep
your distance Abstand halten

distant [ˈdɪstənt] fern

disturbance [dɪˈstɜːbəns] Störung

(to) divide [dɪˈvaɪd] teilen

dizzy [ˈdɪzi] schwindlig

doorbell [ˈdɔːbel] Türklingel

doorframe [ˈdɔːrfreɪm] Türrahmen

doubt [daʊt] (n) Zweifel; (v)
zweifeln

(to) drag [dræg] ziehen

(to) draw [drɔː] zeichnen; ziehen

dreamy [ˈdriːmi] träumerisch

(to) drift [drɪft] (to) drift off to
sleep einschlafen

(to) drill [drɪl] bohren

driver's licence [ˈdraɪvəz laɪsns]
Führerschein

(to) duck [dʌk] sich ducken

dust [dʌst] Staub

dusty [ˈdʌsti] staubig

E

eagle [ˈiːgl] Adler

edge [edʒ] Kante

effect [ɪˈfekt] Auswirkung

effective [ɪˈfektɪv] wirksam,
wirkungsvoll

effectively [ɪˈfektɪvli] im Endeffekt

effort ['efət] Bemühen, Anstrengung

either ['aɪðə] auch nicht

elbow ['elbəʊ] Ellbogen

election [ɪ'lekʃn] Wahl

electricity [ɪˌlek'trɪsəti] Strom(versorgung)

(to) emerge [i'mɜːdʒ] herauskommen

employer [ɪm'plɔɪə] Arbeitgeber/in

(to) encourage [ɪn'kʌrɪdʒ] ermuntern

engineer [ˌendʒɪ'nɪə] Ingenieur/in

(to) enlighten [ɪn'laɪtn] ausklären

(to) enrol [ɪn'rəʊl] anmelden

enthusiastically [ɪnˌθjuːzi'æstɪkli] begeistert

entire [ɪn'taɪə] ganz, gesamt

entirely [ɪn'taɪəli] ganz, vollständig

entrance ['entrəns] Eingang

environment [ɪn'vaɪrənmənt] Umwelt

equipped [ɪ'kwɪpt] vorbereitet

(to) escort [ɪ'skɔːt] begleiten

eternity [ɪ'tɜːnəti] Ewigkeit

eventually [ɪ'ventʃuəli] letztendlich

(to) examine [ɪg'zæmɪn] untersuchen

(to) exchange [ɪks'tʃeɪndʒ]: (to) exchange a look einen Blick tauschen

(to) expand [ɪk'spænd] ausweitern

(to) expel [ɪk'spel] ausschließen

explanation [ˌeksplə'neɪʃn] Erklärung

eyebrow ['aɪbraʊ]: raise an eyebrow eine Augenbraue hochziehen

eyelid ['aɪlɪd] Augenlid

eyewitness ['aɪwɪtnəs] Augenzeuge/in

F

facility [fə'sɪləti]: medical facility medizinische Einrichtung

(to) fail [feɪl] scheitern

(to) fall apart ['fɔːl əpɑːt] zusammenbrechen

familiar [fə'mɪliə] vertraut

faraway ['fɑːrəweɪ] fern

(to) fast-track [fɑːst træk] beschleunigen

fatigue [fə'tiːg] Müdigkeit

favour ['feɪvə] Gunst

fear [fɪə] Angst

fellow ['feləʊ] fellow countryman Landsmann

(to) figure ['fɪgə] denken

fingertip ['fɪŋgətɪp] Fingerspitze

fishing rod ['fɪʃɪŋ rɒd] Angelrute

(to) fit [fɪt] passen

(to) flake off ['fleɪk ɒf] abblättern

(to) flash [flæʃ] aufblitzen

flashing ['flæʃɪŋ] blitzend

flesh [fleʃ] Fleisch

(to) flinch [flɪntʃ] zucken

flow [fləʊ] Strom

(to) flunk [flʌŋk] durchfallen

(to) fold [fəʊld] falten

footbridge ['fʊtbrɪdʒ] Fußgängerbrücke

footstep ['fʊtstep] Schritt

forcefully [ˈfɔːsfəli] kräftig

forehead [ˈfɔːhed] Stirn

forest [ˈfɒrɪst] Wald

forever [fərˈevə] für immer

(to) forgive [fəˈgɪv] vergeben

former [ˈfɔːmə] ehemalig

fortress [ˈfɔːtrəs] Festung

fortunately [ˈfɔːtʃənətli] glücklicherweise

fraction [ˈfrækʃn] Bruchteil

(to) frame [ˈfreɪm] umrahmen

frankness [ˈfræŋknəs] Offenheit

(to) freeze [friːz] frieren (freeze, froze, frozen)

fried [fraɪd] gebraten

frigging [ˈfrɪgɪŋ] verdammt

frosted glass [ˈfrɒstɪd glɑːs] Milchglas

(to) frown [fraʊn] die Stirn runzeln

frying pan [ˈfraɪŋ pæn] Bratpfanne

fugitive [ˈfjuːdʒətɪv] Flüchtige(r)

further [fɜːðə] weiter, zusätzlich

fuss [fʌs] Aufregung

G

(to) gain [geɪn] gewinnen

(to) gather [ˈgæðə] sich sammeln

gaze [geɪz] (n) Blick; (v) anstarren

gears [gɪəz] Gänge

generosity [ˌdʒenəˈrɒsəti] Großzügigkeit

gently [ˈdʒentli] sanft

genuinely [ˈdʒenjuɪnli] wirklich

(to) get past [get ˈpɑːst] vorbeikommen

gift [gɪft] Geschenk

(to) giggle [ˈgɪgl] kichern

glance [glɑːns]: sneak a glance einen Blick erhaschen; throw a glance einen Blick werfen; (v) einen Blick werfen

(to) gleam [gliːm] leuchten

goddam [ˈgɒddæm] verdampt

gonna [ˈgənə] = going to

goods [gʊdz] Waren, Güter

(to) grab [græb] greifen

(to) grant [grɑːnt] erteilen

greeting [ˈgriːtɪŋ] Begrüßung

grimly [ˈgrɪmli] trostlos

grip [grɪp] (n) Griff; (v) fassen

(to) grit [grɪt] zusammenbeißen

(to) growl [graʊl] knurren

guard [gɑːd] Wächter

guilty [ˈgɪlti] schuldig

gun [gʌn] Gewehr

gunshot [ˈgʌnʃɒt] Schüsse

H

habitat [ˈhæbɪtæt] Lebensraum

hair [heə] Haar

haircut [ˈheəkʌt] Haarschnitt

(to) hand over [hænd ˈəʊvə] übergeben

hand-written [ˈhændrɪtn] handschriftlich

(to) handle [ˈhændl] mit etwas umgehen

harbour [ˈhɑːbə] Hafen

(to) harden [ˈhɑːdn] sich verhärten

hardly [ˈhɑːdli] kaum

(to) harm [hɑːm] schaden

hatred [ˈheɪtrɪd] Hass

headless [ˈhedləs] kopflos

headphones [ˈhedfəʊnz] Kopfhörer

heel [hiːl] Schuhabsatz
hell [hel] Höhle
helpless ['helpləs] hilflos
(to) hesitate ['hezɪteɪt] zögern
hip [hɪp] Hüfte
homely ['həʊmli] gemütlich
(to) honour ['ɒnə] ehren
horizon [həˈraɪzn] Horizont
hostage ['hɒstɪdʒ] Geisel/in
(to) hover ['hɒvə] schweben
huddled up ['hʌdld ʌp] sich
    zusammengekauert
(to) hum [hʌm] summen
human ['hjuːmən] Mensch
human being [hjuːmən 'biːɪŋ]
    Mensch
human rights [hjuːmən 'raɪtz]
    Menschenrechte
humanity [hjuːˈmænəti] Mensch-
    lichkeit
humid ['hjuːmɪd] feucht
humidity [hjuːˈmɪdəti] Luft-
    feuchtigkeit
humiliating [hjuːˈmɪlieɪtɪŋ]
    demütigend
(to) hurry ['hʌri] sich beeilen
hushed [hʌʃt] gedämpft
hut [hʌt] Hütte
hype [haɪp] Rummel

I

ID [ˌaɪ 'diː] Identitätskarte, Ausweis
immediately [ɪˈmiːdiətli] sofort
impatience [ɪmˈpeɪʃns] Ungeduld
imperative [ɪmˈperətɪv] zwingend
impossible [ɪmˈpɒsəbl] unmöglich
impression [ɪmˈpreʃn] Eindruck

impressive [ɪmˈpresɪv]
    beeindruckend
improper [ɪmˈprɒpə] unsachgemäß
    Verhalten
improvement [ɪmˈpruːvmənt]
    Verbesserung
inconspicuously [ˌɪnkənˈspɪkjuəsli]
    unauffällig
increased [ɪnˈkriːst] erhöht
indifference [ɪnˈdɪfrəns] Gleich-
    gültigkeit
(to) infuriate [ɪnˈfjʊərieɪt] wütend
    machen
injection [ɪnˈdʒekʃn] Spritze
injustice [ɪnˈdʒʌstɪs] Ungerech-
    tigkeit
inquiry [ɪnˈkwaɪəri] Untersuchung
(to) insist [ɪnˈsɪst] beharren
(to) inspect [ɪnˈspekt] untersuchen
intercom ['ɪntəkɒm] Sprechanlage
interference [ˌɪntəˈfɪərəns] Eingriff,
    Intervention
(to) interrupt [ˌɪntəˈrʌpt] unter-
    brechen
intricate ['ɪntrɪkət] komplex
(to) invent [ɪnˈvent] erfinden
irresponsible [ˌɪrɪˈspɒnsəbl] unver-
    antwortlich

J

juicy ['dʒuːsi] saftig
justice ['dʒʌstɪs] Gerechtigkeit
(to) justify [dʒʌstɪfaɪ] rechtfertigen

K

(to) kidnap ['kɪdnæp] entführen
knowledge ['nɒlɪdʒ] Wissen

L

lamb [læm] Lamm

landmark [ˈlændmɑːk] Wahr-
zeichen

(to) last [lɑːst] dauern

laughter [ˈlɑːftə] Lachen

lawyer [ˈlɔːjə] Anwalt/Anwältin

(to) lead [liːd] führen (lead, led,
led)

lead-up [ˈliːd ʌp] Vorfeld,
Abschlussphase

leaf [liːf] Blatt

leftovers [ˈleftəʊvəz] Essensreste

leper [ˈlepə] Aussätzige(r)

(to) let down [let ˈdaʊn] im Stich
lassen

liable [ˈlaɪəbl] strafbar

liar [ˈlaɪə] Lügner/in

lid [lɪd] Deckel

lifelessly [ˈlaɪfləsli] leblos

lizard [ˈlɪzəd] Eidechse

(to) loathe [ləʊð] verabscheuen

local [ˈləʊkl] Einheimische(r)

located [ləʊˈkeɪtɪd]: (to) be
located sich befinden

lock [lɒk] (n) Schloss; (v) schließen

(to) lock up [ˈlɒk ʌp] einsperren

loggerheads [ˈlɒgəhedz]: be at loggerheads sich in den Haaren
liegen

long-term [lɒŋ ˈtɜːm] langfristig

loose [luːs] locker

lord [lɔːd] Herr

loudspeaker [ˌlaʊdˈspiːkə] Laut-
sprecher

lounge [laʊndʒ] Wohnzimmer

(to) lower [ˈləʊə] leiser machen

lump [lʌmp] Klumpen, Masse

M

madness [ˈmædnəs] Wahnsinn

magical [ˈmædʒɪkl] zauberhaft

mainland [ˈmeɪnlænd] Festland

mainly [ˈmeɪnli] vor allem

major [ˈmeɪdʒə] groß

male [meɪl] Mann

mangrove [ˈmæŋgrəʊv]
Mangrovenbaum

masterpiece [ˈmɑːstəpiːs] Meister-
werk

mat [mæt] Matte

matching [ˈmætʃɪŋ] passend

mate [meɪt] Freund

mayor [meə] Bürgermeister/in

meantime [ˈmiːntaɪm] Zwischen-
zeit

meatball [ˈmiːtbɔːl] Fleischklops

medical facility [medɪkl fəˈsɪləti]
medizinische Einrichtung

medicine [ˈmedsn] Medikament

memory [ˈmeməri] Erinnerung

mental [ˈmentl] psychisch

(to) mention [ˈmenʃn] erwähnen

mercy [ˈmɜːsi] Gnade

merry [ˈmeri] fröhlich; besser

meteoric [ˌmiːtiˈɒrɪk] rasant

mid-sentence [mɪd ˈsentəns] mit-
ten im Satz

midday [ˌmɪdˈdeɪ] Mittag

(to) migrate [maɪˈgreɪt] migrieren

mind [maɪnd] Geist, Kopf

minor [ˈmaɪnə] Minderjährige(r)

miracle [ˈmɪrəkl] Wunder

mix [mɪks] Mischung

modern-day [mɒdn ˈdeɪ] aktuell
moonless [ˈmuːnləs] mondlos
mosquito [məˈskiːtəʊ] Mücke
mould [məʊld] Schimmel
murderer [ˈmɜːdərə] Mörder/in
mute [mjuːt] stumm

N

nap [næp] Nickerchen
nationality [ˌnæʃəˈnæləti] Staats-
angehörigkeit
nationwide [ˌneɪʃnˈwaɪd] landes-
weit
natural [ˈnætʃrəl] (adj) Natur-; (n)
Naturtalent
naughty [ˈnɔːti] böse
neat [niːt] ordentlich
neck [nek] Hals
negotiator [nɪˈgəʊʃieɪtə] Vermitt-
ler/in, Verhandlungsführer/in
neither [ˈnaɪðə] keiner
nerve-wracking [ˈnɜːv ræktŋ]
nervenaufreibende
nerves [nɜːvz]: (to) get on sb.'s
nerves auf die Nerven gehen
(to) nibble [ˈnɪbl] knabbern
nightmare [ˈnaɪtmeə] Albtraum
nor [nɔː] auch nicht
nostril [ˈnɒstrəl] Nasenloch

O

(to) obey [əˈbeɪ] gehorchen
obligation [ˌɒblɪˈgeɪʃn] Verpflich-
tung
obliged [əˈblaɪdʒd] gezwungen
occasionally [əˈkeɪʒnəli] gelegen-
tlich

(to) occur [əˈkɜː] (to) occur to sb.
jdm. einfallen
officer [ˈɒfɪsə] Offizier
official [əˈfɪʃl] Vertreter/in
offshore [ˌɒfˈʃɔː] außerhalb von
Australien
ointment [ˈɔɪntmənt] Salbe
opponent [əˈpəʊnənt] Gegner/in
opportunity [ˌɒpəˈtjuːnəti]
Gelegenheit
otherwise [ˈʌðəwaɪz] sonst
Outback [ˈaʊtbæk]: the Outback
das Hinterland (Australien)
(to) outline [ˈaʊtlaɪn] schildern
(to) outlive [ˌaʊtˈlɪv] überleben
outrage [ˈaʊtreɪdʒ] Empörung
overboard [ˈəʊvəbɔːd] über Bord
(to) overhear [ˌəʊvəˈhɪə] mithören
own [əʊn]: on your own alleine
oxygen [ˈɒksɪdʒən] Sauerstoff

P

(to) pace [peɪs] schreiten
padlock [ˈpædlɒk] (n) Schloss; (v)
mit einem Schloss verschließen
pale [peɪl] blass
palm [pɑːm] Handfläche
palm tree [ˈpɑːm triː] Palme
pan [pæn] Pfanne
paramedic [ˌpærəˈmedɪk]
Rettungssanitäter/in
parrot [ˈpærət] Papagei
passport [ˈpɑːspɔːt] Reisepass
pat [pæt] Klaps
patience [ˈpeɪʃns] Geduld
patrol car [pəˈtrəʊl kə] Streifen-
wagen

(to) pause [pɔːz] innehalten

peace [piːs] Frieden

peaceful [ˈpiːsfl] friedlich

perplexed [pəˈplekst] ratlos

(to) persuade [pəˈsweɪd] überzeugen

petal [ˈpetl] Blütenblatt

physically [ˈfɪzɪkli] physisch

pickles [ˈpɪkəlz] eingelegtes Gemüse

(to) piece together [ˈpiːs təgeðə] zusammenstückeln

pile [paɪl] Stapel

pinball machine [ˈpɪnbɔːl məˈʃiːn] Flipperautomat

pineapple [ˈpaɪnæpl] Ananas

(to) place [pleɪs] legen

plains [pleɪnz] Ebenen

plank [plæŋk] Brett

plenty of [ˈplenti əv] viel

(to) point out [pɔɪnt ˈaʊt] weisen

policeman/policewoman [pəˈliːsmən/pəˈliːswʊmən] Polizist/in

politician [ˌpɒləˈtɪʃn] Politiker/in

(to) pop around [pɒp əˈraʊnd] vorbeischauen

(to) pose [pəʊz] stellen

pot [pɒt] Topf

(to) pound [paʊnd] klopfen

(to) pour [pɔː] strömen

practicality [ˌpræktɪˈkæləti] Praktikabilität

(to) praise [preɪz] loben

(to) pray [preɪ] beten

predecessor [ˈpriːdɪsesə] Vorgänger/in

(to) predict [prɪˈdɪkt] vorhersagen

(to) preoccupy [priˈɒkjupaɪ] beschäftigen

press [pres] (n) Presse; (v) drücken

(to) press charges [pres ˈtʃɑːdʒəz] Anklage erheben

primary school [ˈpraɪməri skuːl] Grundschule

procedure [prəˈsiːdʒə] Vorgehen

process [ˈprəʊses] (v) bearbeiten, abwickeln; (n) Verfahren

proof [pruːf] Beweis

(to) prop [prɒp] stützen

property [ˈprɒpəti] Eigentum

protection [prəˈtekʃn] Schutz

protestor [prəˈtestə] Demostrant/in

(to) provide [prəˈvaɪd] bieten

public [ˈpʌblɪk] (adj) öffentlich; (to) make sth. public etwas bekannt machen; (n) Publikum

public services [pʌblɪk ˈsɜːvɪsəs] öffentliche Dienste

(to) punish [ˈpʌnɪʃ] bestrafen

pupil [ˈpjuːpl] Schüler/in

Q

quarter [ˈkwɔːtə] Viertel

queue [kjuː] Schlange

R

(to) raise [reɪz] erhöhen

raisin [ˈreɪzn] Rosine

rather [ˈrɑːðə] eher

(to) rattle [ˈrætl] rütteln

(to) realise [ˈriːəlaɪz] begreifen, wahrnehmen

rear-view mirror [rɪə vjuː ˈmɪrə] Rückspiegel

reasonable [ˈriːznəbl] vernünftig

reassurance [ˌriːəˈʃʊərəns] Vergewisserung

reception committee [rɪˈsepʃn kəmɪti] Empfangskomitee

(to) reckon [ˈrekən] schätzen, meinen

(to) recognise [ˈrekəgnaɪz] erkennen

rectangle [ˈrektæŋgl] Rechteck

red-handed [red ˈhændɪd]: catch sb. red-handed jdn. bei der Tat ergreifen

refugee [ˌrefjuˈdʒiː] Flüchtling

(to) refuse [rɪˈfjuːz] verweigern

(to) regret [rɪˈgret] Reue

(to) rehearse [rɪˈhɜːs] üben

(to) reject [rɪˈdʒekt] ablehnen

relations [rɪˈleɪʃnz] Beziehungen

relative [ˈrelətɪv] Verwandte(r)

(to) release [rɪˈliːs] freilassen

relieved [rɪˈliːvd] erleichtert

(to) relocate [ˌriːləʊˈkeɪt] verlegen

reluctantly [rɪˈlʌktəntli] wiederwillig

(to) remain [rɪˈmeɪn] bleiben

remains [rɪˈmeɪnz] Trümmer

remote [rɪˈməʊt] (n) Fernbedienung; (v) abgelegen

removal [rɪˈmuːvl] Verlagerung

(to) remove [rɪˈmuːv] entfernen

reply (n) [rɪˈplaɪ] Antwort; (v) antworten

reserved [rɪˈzɜːvd] zurückhaltend

resettlement [ˌriːˈsetlmənt] Umsiedlung

(to) reshape [ˌriːˈʃeɪp] umstalten

(to) resist [rɪˈzɪst] sich wehren

(to) respond [rɪˈspɒnd] reagieren

responsibility [rɪˌspɒnsəˈbɪləti] Verantwortung

resting place [ˈrestɪŋ pleɪs] Rastplatz

(to) result [rɪˈzʌlt]: (to) result in sth. zu etwas führen

(to) return [rɪˈtɜːn] zurückkehren

reunification [riːjuːnɪfɪˈkeɪʃn] Zusammenführung

reverse [rɪˈvɜːs] Rückwärtsgang

(to) revise [rɪˈvaɪz] lernen

rice [raɪs] Reis

riddle [ˈrɪdl] Rätsel

ringleader [ˈrɪŋliːdə] Anführer/in

riot gear [ˈraɪət gɪə] Schutzmontur

(to) rip apart [rɪp əˈpɑːt] auseinanderreißen

(to) rip off [rɪp ˈɒf] losreißen

rise [raɪz] (n) Aufstieg; (v) aufsteigen (rise, rose, risen)

roadside [ˈrəʊdsaɪd] Straßenseite

(to) roar [rɔː] brüllen

(to) rock [rɒk] schaukeln; (to) rock the boat das Boot ins Wanken bringen

rock-bottom [rɒk ˈbɒtəm] Tiefpunkt, Nullpunkt

rooftop [ˈruːftɒp] Dach

row [raʊ] Streit

row [rəʊ] Reihe

(to) rub [rʌb] reiben

(to) ruffle [ˈrʌfl] sträuben

S

(to) sail [seɪl] segeln

salty [ˈsɔːlti] salzig

scale [skeɪl] Schuppen

scar [skɑː] Narbe

(to) schedule [ˈʃedʒuːl] planen

schoolbag [ˈskuːlbæg] Schultasche

schoolyard [ˈskuːljɑːd] Schulhof

scientist [ˈsaɪəntɪst] Wissen-
schaftler/in

scuffle [ˈskʌfl] Rauferei

scum [skʌm] Abschaum

sec [sek] = second

secondary school [ˈsekəndri skuːl]
Sekundärschule

seldom [ˈseldəm] selten

(to) select [sɪˈlekt] auswählen

selection [sɪˈlekʃn] Auswahl

sense [sens] (n) Sinn; (v) spüren

sensitive [ˈsensətɪv] empfindlich

(to) separate [ˈsepəreɪt] sich trennen; trennen

serious [ˈsɪəriəs] ernst

services [ˈsɜːvɪsəs] Dienste

set-up [ˈset ʌp] Spiel

(to) sew up [səʊ] zunähen (sew,
sewed, sewn)

(to) shake [ʃeɪk] zittern, schütteln

shakily [ˈʃeɪkɪli] schwankend

(to) shape [ʃeɪp] gestalten

sheet [ʃiːt] Bettlacken

shelter [ˈʃeltə] Schutz

(to) shield [ʃiːld] abschirmen

shitty [ˈʃɪti] beschissen

(to) shoot [ʃuːt] schießen; bestür-
men

shortly [ˈʃɔːtli] kurz

shower [ˈʃaʊə] Dusche

(to) shrug [ʃrʌg]: (to) shrug your
shoulders die Achseln zucken

(to) shut [ʃʌt]: (to) slam sth. shut
etwas zuschlagen

sickness [ˈsɪknəs] Krankheit

(to) sigh [saɪ] seufzen

silent [ˈsaɪlənt] still

siren [ˈsaɪrən] Sirene

skull [skʌl] Schädel

(to) slam [slæm]: (to) slam sth.
shut etwas zuschlagen

slap [slæp] schlagen

slender [ˈslendə] schmal

slightly [ˈslaɪtli] ein wenig

(to) slip [slɪp] stecken

(to) slip back [slɪp ˈbæk] hinein-
schleichen

(to) slip out [slɪp ˈaʊt] hin-
ausschleichen

(to) slurp [slɜːp] schlürfen

slurred [slɜːd] verwaschen

smelly [ˈsmeli] stinkend

smooth [smuːð] glatt

(to) smuggle [ˈsmʌgl] schmuggeln

(to) snap [snæp] bellen

(to) sneak a glance [sniːk ə ˈglɑːns]
einen Blick erhaschen

sneaky [ˈsniːki] hinterlistig

(to) sniff [snɪf] schnüppern

(to) snort [snɔːt] schnauben

snowball [ˈsnəʊbɔːl] lawinenartig
anwachsen

(to) soak up [səʊk ˈʌp] aufsaugen

(to) sob [sɒb] schluchzen

soft [sɒft] sanft

soft drink ['sɒft drɪŋk] alkohol-
freies Getränk
(to) solve [sɒlv] lösen
sorrow ['sɒrəʊ] Trauer
(to) sort out [sɔːt 'aʊt] in Ordnung
bringen
soul [səʊl] Seele
source [sɔːs] Quelle
sovereign ['sɒvrɪn] souverän,
höheitlich
spam [spæm] Art Schinkenfleisch
spare ribs [speə rɪb] Rippchen
(to) sparkle ['spɑːkl] funkeln
sparrow ['spærəʊ] Spatz
species ['spiːʃiːz] Art
speckled ['spekld] befleckt
speechless ['spiːtʃləs] sprachlos
spicy ['spaɪsi] scharf
(to) spin [spɪn] durchdrehen
(to) spit [spɪt] spucken
(to) spread [spred] sich verbreiten
(to) squeal [skwiːl] quietschen
(to) squeeze [skwiːz] drücken
(to) squint [skwɪnt] blinzeln
(to) stab [stæb] erstechen
stage [steɪdʒ] (n) Podium, Bühne;
(v) inszenieren
stairwell ['steəwel] Treppenhaus
(to) step back [step 'bæk] zurück-
treten
(to) step into [step 'ɪntu] hinein-
treten
sternly ['stɜːnli] ernst
stew [stjuː] Eintopf
stiff [stɪf] steif
storey ['stɔːri] Stockwerk
storm [stɔːm] Sturm

stove [stəʊv] Herd
straight [streɪt] direkt
straightaway [ˌstreɪtə'weɪ] sofort
stranger ['streɪndʒə] Fremde(r)
strap [stræp] Riemen
(to) stretch [stretʃ] sich erstrecken
strikingly ['straɪkɪŋli] auffallend
suburb ['sʌbɜːb] Vorort
(to) suffocate ['sʌfəkeɪt] ersticken
suggestion [sə'dʒestʃən] Vorschlag
suit [suːt] Anzug
sundown ['sʌndaʊn] Sonnen-
untergang
supplies [sə'plaɪz] Vorräte
surrounded [sə'raʊndɪd] umgeben
survival [sə'vaɪvl] Überleben
(to) survive [sə'vaɪv] überleben
suspicion [sə'spɪʃn] Verdacht
sustainable [sə'steɪnəbl] haltbar
(to) swallow ['swɒləʊ] schlucken
(to) sweat [swet] schwitzen
(to) sweep [swiːp] fegen
(to) sweep apart [swiːp ə'pɑːt]
auseinanderfegen
(to) swell up [swell 'ʌp] auf-
schwellen
(to) swirl [swɜːl] wirbeln
(to) swoop [swuːp] schnappen
sympathy ['sɪmpəθi] Mitgefühl,
Verständnis

T

(to) taste [teɪst] schmecken
temporary ['temprəri] befristet
tense [tens] angespannt
(to) thank [θæŋk] danken
thief [θiːf] Dieb/in

thread [θred] Faden

thrill [θrɪl] Nervenkitzel

thumb [θʌm] Daumen

thunderstorm [ˈθʌndəstɔːm] Gewitter

tidal wave [ˈtaɪdl weɪv] Flutwelle

(to) tie [taɪ] binden

(to) tighten [ˈtaɪtn] festigen

tile [taɪl] Fliese

tin opener [tɪn ˈəʊpnə] Dosenöffner

(to) tip [tɪp] kippen

to and fro [ˈtu ənd ˈfrəʊ] hin und her

tone [təʊn] Umgangston

toothache [ˈtuːθeɪk] Zahnschmerzen

toothbrush [ˈtuːθbrʌʃ] Zahnbürste

torn [tɔːn] zerrissen

totally [ˈtəʊtəli] auf jeden Fall

touch [ˈtʌtʃ]: (to) get in touch with sb. mit jdm. Kontakt aufnehmen; (v) anfassen, berühren

(to) trace [treɪs] zurückverfolgen

trading [ˈtreɪdɪŋ] Handels-

(to) transfer [trænsˈfɜː] überstellen

tray [treɪ] Tablett

(to) treat [triːt] behandeln

treatment [ˈtriːtmənt] Behandlung

(to) trespass [ˈtrespəs] illegal betreten

(to) trickle [ˈtrɪkl] tröpfeln

tricky [ˈtrɪki] knifflig

Triple Zero [trɪpl ˈzɪərəʊ] Nummer der Notdienste

triumphant [traɪˈʌmfənt] siegreich

trunk [trʌŋk] Stamm

tub [tʌb] Becher

(to) turn away [tɜːn əˈweɪ] sich wegdrehen

(to) turn sb. away [tɜːn əˈweɪ] jdn. abweisen

(to) turn up [tɜːn ˈʌp] auftauchen

twisted [ˈtwɪstɪd] verdreht

U

unable [ʌnˈeɪbl] nicht in der Lage (sein)

unaccompanied [ʌnəˈkʌmpənid] unbegleitet

unbearably [ʌnˈbeərəbli] unerträglich

uncomfortable [ʌnˈkʌmftəbl] unangenehm

(to) underestimate [ʌndərˈestimeɪt] unterschätzen

(to) undertake [ʌndəˈteɪk] unternehmen

unfamiliar [ʌnfəˈmɪliə] unbekannt

unharmed [ʌnˈhɑːmd] unversehrt

(to) unlock [ʌnˈlɒk] entriegeln

unnecessarily [ʌnˈnesəsərəli] unnötigerweise

(to) unpack [ʌnˈpæk] auspacken

(to) unroll [ʌnˈrəʊl] ausrollen

untouched [ʌnˈtʌtʃt] unberührt

update [ʌpˈdeɪt] Aktualisierung, Lagerbericht

upset [ʌpˈset] aufgebracht

urgent [ˈɜːdʒənt] dringend

V

values [ˈvæljuːz] Werte

various [ˈveəriəs] verschieden

Vegemite [ˈvedʒɪmaɪt] Hefe-
extraktaufstrich

velvety [ˈvelvəti] samtig

(to) vomit [ˈvɒmɪt] erbrechen

voyage [ˈvɔɪɪdʒ] Reise

vulnerable [ˈvʌlnərəbl] gefährdet

W

(to) waft [wɒft] wehen

wanna [ˈwɒnə] = want to

(to) warm [wɔːm] wärmen

wasteful [ˈweɪstfl] verschwende-
risch

(to) wear off [weə ˈɒf] nachlassen

weed [wiːd] Gras

weed-buddy [ˈwiːd bʌdi] Kumpel
mit dem man Joints raucht

wharf [wɔːf] Anlegestelle

whatever [wɒtˈevə] was immer

wherever [weərˈevə] wo immer

whether [ˈweðə] ob

whip [wɪp] (n) Peitsche; (v) peit-
schen

(to) widen [ˈwaɪdn] sich weiten

windswept [ˈwɪndswept] wind-
gepeitscht

wing [wɪŋ] Flügel; (to) take sb.
under your wing jdn. unter
seine Fittiche nehmen

(to) wipe [waɪp] wischen

withdrawal [wɪðˈdrɔːəl] Rücktritt

within [wɪˈðɪn] innerhalb

wooden [ˈwʊdn] Holz-

worldwide [ˈwɜːldwaɪd] weltweit

wound [wuːnd] Wunde

(to) wrap [ræp] verpacken

wrist [rɪst] Handgelenk

Z

zip [zɪp] Reißverschluss

(to) zip up [ˈzɪp ʌp] verschließen

Check your understanding

Part One

Sections	Tasks	
1	1	Compare the ideas of heaven and hell.
2	1	Explain who the narrator of the first section (in italics) is.
3–5	1	Explain the situation of the narrators in the sections in italics and those in normal typeface.
	2	Explain why Coop refuses to tell his dad about Bashir.
6	1	From all that you have read so far, write character descriptions of Bashir and Coop.
7	1	Describe Bashir's experiences.
	2	Do you think he was right to go to Australia? Explain your answer.
8	1	Explain how the people in the camp feel.
	2	What do you think Coop's dad will do?
9	1	Why did Saba's dad sew his lips together?
10	1	What do you think Mr Jackson's plans are?
11	1	Describe Mr Jackson's plan. What do you think of it?
12–14	1	What do we learn of Australia's policy towards refugees?
	2	How do the individual members of the Jackson family react to Bashir?
	3	Describe in a few sentences what happened at the TV debate.

15   1 From everything you have read so far state what you think will happen to Bashir and to the Jackson family.

Part Two

Sections	Tasks
1	1 Describe what has happened to Bashir.
	2 How safe is he in the camp?
2	1 Why does Coop decide to take action?
	2 To what extent are his fears about the camp justified?
	3 Describe Coop's plan of action.
3–4	1 Both Bashir and Coop take action. Evaluate how effective their actions are.
5	1 Explain the comedown both boys have.
6	1 Summarize the events that lead to Bashir moving to Darwin.